Second Edition

The Complete
Lean Enterprise

Value Stream Mapping for Office and Services

Second Edition

The Complete Lean Enterprise

Value Stream Mapping for Office and Services

Beau Keyte • Drew A. Locher

CRC Press
Taylor & Francis Group
Boca Raton London New York

CRC Press is an imprint of the
Taylor & Francis Group, an **informa** business

A PRODUCTIVITY PRESS BOOK

CRC Press
Taylor & Francis Group
6000 Broken Sound Parkway NW, Suite 300
Boca Raton, FL 33487-2742

Printed on acid-free paper
Version Date: 20150629

International Standard Book Number-13: 978-1-4822-0613-5 (Paperback)

Library of Congress Cataloging-in-Publication Data

Keyte, Beau, author.
  The complete lean enterprise : value stream mapping for office and services / Beau Keyte and Drew A. Locher. -- Second edition.
      pages cm
  Includes bibliographical references and index.
    ISBN 978-1-4822-0613-5 (alk. paper)
    1. Organizational effectiveness. 2. Industrial efficiency. 3. Office management--Cost control. 4. Industrial management--Cost effectiveness. 5. Value added. I. Locher, Drew, author. II. Title.

HD58.9.K455 2015
651.3--dc23   2015024827

**Visit the Taylor & Francis Web site at
http://www.taylorandfrancis.com**

**and the CRC Press Web site at
http://www.crcpress.com**

To my dad and Debi, whose constant love and support have carried me through these years and allowed me to chase my dream. And to all the organizations I've worked with that implicitly provided learning laboratories to move our collective thinking forward.

Beau Keyte

To my wife Eileen, who has stood by me for all these many years. You have always been supportive through all of the time away from home and through the good times and bad. I love, respect, and appreciate you. Thank you for being there with me on life's journey.

Drew A. Locher

Contents

Foreword

An alternative title for this book could be *Waste in the Office: The Final Lean Frontier.* Beau Keyte and Drew A. Locher have accomplished an ambitious task—one that can benefit anyone concerned with creating maximum value for customers with as little waste as possible.

How much waste is there in an enterprise? Stated differently, what percent of activities undertaken by each of us every day actually contribute toward the creation of value for our customers? When we ask how many of our actions directly provide value for our customers, the answer is loud and clear: painfully little.

That is where Beau and Drew come in with this book. Just as *Learning to See* introduced a fresh set of lenses through which to view the manufacturing world, Beau and Drew expand the use of the now-proven Value Stream Mapping (VSM) tool to indirect support operations, and services, locations, and sources of so much waste. VSM as introduced by Beau and Drew seeks to enable users to see administrative and service waste, identify its sources, and develop a future state that eliminates it so that scarce resources can then be focused on those activities truly necessary to create value.

You could find no two more experienced guides for this journey than the well-traveled Beau and Drew. Beau and Drew have been teaming together to teach workshops on the topic for years at the Lean Enterprise Institute, NIST MEP, universities, and for corporations large and small. Their collective experience covers a wide range of enterprises and industries: automotive OEMs and suppliers, aerospace, electronics, consumer perishables, information technology, healthcare, financial institutions, and more.

So, grab your pencils and paper and your walking shoes. The opportunities that present themselves as you learn to peel away the obscurity of administrative work will be tremendous. It's time to get started.

Dan Jones
Ross-on-Wye, England

John Shook
Ann Arbor, Michigan, USA

Acknowledgments

This new version has benefitted from very different influences, which have enriched our learning and, hopefully through this book, yours! The socialization focus was created out of an extraordinary opportunity to work with the Michigan Hospital Association (MHA) when given the challenge of creating a learning environment for 62 different hospital teams at once. We have Sam Watson and Brittany Bogan at MHA to thank for their trust and support as we learned how to develop great ways to engage large segments of organizations in addition to leveraging the learning between teams. What a great experience!

The shift in the future state mapping began as experiments with clients in 2005 and has become a staple in our consulting that helps provide a real eye opener for those on a transformational path. The fundamental shift in the visual management system and its developmental coaching was greatly influenced by the philosophy and support of the Gestalt International Studies Center (GISC) and Edgar Schein through his book *Helping*.

Finally, we had great sounding boards both when things went well and when there were significant challenges. Beau thanks Brent Wahba, Terry Barnhart, and his lifelong coach and trusted advisor, Deb, for this ongoing support. Drew acknowledges all of the organizations with whom he has worked. We just do the best we can to convey the concepts. These organizations are the ones that determine how best to adapt them to meet their specific needs, and nothing brings us more joy than when they accomplish this. They are the true innovators. He also acknowledges his coauthor Beau Keyte for his patience over the two-plus years it took to complete this edition. Much has happened personally over this time, and his support throughout is greatly appreciated.

We also acknowledge our editor, Kirsten Miller, who is always a pleasure to work with to hone our message and teaching.

Authors

Beau Keyte learned very early on about the uniqueness of people, and by extension, the uniqueness of every organization. He was raised in tiny Bradford, Pennsylvania, where his home was part of an exchange program that brought individuals from literally the four corners of the globe to live with his family for brief periods. "By the time I was 15," he says, "we had hosted 12–15 exchange students in our home, and I had even taught a Kuwaiti teenager to speak English."

He also learned a great deal from his father, a welding engineer in high demand after World War II, who ran four manufacturing plants from his base at the Bradford plant. "He traveled a lot to the other plants in Alabama and Belgium," says Beau. "And even though he was in management, he got along great with the unions for one simple reason. He made a point of getting to know everyone. They and their opinions mattered very much to him."

With his background as a guide and his father as a role model, Beau set out to build a career, one that not surprisingly has required him to adapt quickly to different corporate cultures, and get to know the people in them. After graduating with a BS in engineering from the University of Michigan, Beau continued to learn and add tools to his consulting kit to make him more effective in these endeavors, acquiring an MBA and gaining invaluable experience in a variety of companies.

In 2003, he was hand-picked to work on a high-profile General Motors project led by Lean thinking guru and pioneer John Shook. After finishing their work together with GM, John, Beau, and five others formed the core of the Lean Transformations Group (LTG). Beau left LTG in 2014 and continues his work through the Keyte Group.

Beau truly loves what he does, helping organizations find their own way by doing what he does best—listening, teaching, and facilitating. His interactions are high energy and effective, and yet he says he is actually doing his best work when he seems invisible. In fact, one of his all-time favorite moments involved a client who told him that the staff had learned more from each other in their session together than they did from him. "It made me feel good that they were comfortable telling me that," he says, "and, it made me better understand how effective one can be without grabbing the spotlight. It was great to hear because I strive to make that happen every time."

When asked about the one thing he would change in companies these days, he echoes his father's democratic view of the importance and value of everyone: "If I could, I'd change management's perceptions about front-line people and affirm for them what a great resource they can be if you just give them a chance and empower them to help solve their problems. A big part of why I love the Lean principles is that they aspire to do just that."

Beau lives in Ann Arbor, Michigan, with wife Debi.

Beau can be reached on LinkedIn or at www.keytegroup.com.

Drew A. Locher first became involved in the development and delivery of innovative business improvement programs while working for General Electric in the 1980s. Since leaving GE in 1990 and forming Change Management Associates (CMA), he has provided operational excellence and organizational development services to industrial and service organizations representing a wide variety of industries including healthcare, transportation, distribution, education, financial services, and manufacturing.

In 2004, Drew coauthored the first edition of *The Complete Lean Enterprise: Value Stream Mapping for Administrative and Office Processes*. The book won a 2005 Shingo Prize for Research. In 2008 he published a book titled *Value Stream Mapping for Lean Development: A How-to Guide for Streamlining Time to Market*. His third book, titled *Lean Office and Service Simplified*, was released February 2011, and received a Shingo Prize for Research in 2012. Drew's most recent book is titled *Unleashing the Power of 3P: The Key to Breakthrough Results*. He is a frequent speaker at conferences in the United States and abroad on the subject of Lean Enterprise and Enterprise Excellence.

Drew has been a faculty member at the Lean Enterprise Institute since 2001. He is on the University of Michigan's Integrative Systems + Design (ISD) instruction team for Improvement/Coaching Kata and Lean Leadership programs. Drew is also a faculty member of the Thedacare Center for Healthcare Value. He has always viewed his role as teacher first and believes that once people understand the concepts, they can determine how best to adapt them to meet their specific needs as part of a "learn by doing approach." Drew lives in Mount Laurel, New Jersey, with his wife Eileen.

Drew can be reached on LinkedIn or at www.cma4results.com.

Introduction

Why Another Book, and Why Now?

We started our office value stream mapping effort in earnest only a few weeks after *Learning to See* hit the market a long time ago. It took about six years for us to feel comfortable writing our first edition of *The Complete Lean Enterprise*, but it was worth the wait as it was awarded the first Shingo Prize for discussions about office work and flow. While the first edition appears to have helped a great many people, Lean thinking continues to shift and evolve as the movement removes its Toyota training wheels and learns how to create its own path. We've been excited and humbled to see many companies make value stream mapping, thinking, and management a part of what they believe will help deliver customer value. And, in parallel, they allow the value creators in their organization to learn how to design better flow that removes much of the chaos of legacy systems. As a result, these value creators have a chance to catch their collective breaths and enjoy what they are doing: learning to improve work and doing improved work!

So, why worry about improving on a good thing and write this second edition? We have two compelling reasons to do this. The first tells us *why another book*: we believe in PDCA (Plan–Do–Check–Act) and the PDCA model keeps us thinking about improvements to our thinking and methodology. Supporting this is a decade-old suggestion made by Dan Jones when he was reviewing the manuscript for our first edition: he suggested we include service industry examples in the book. We chose not to do this as we saw service knowledge being shared in a separate book … that was never written! Ten years later we still feel the need to talk and write about this important segment of our global economy.

The second reason for this book answers the question *why now?* We've been fortunate and diligent enough to apply PDCA to our own thinking and methods and have learned how to improve our 2004 methodology through the success of our clients' efforts. Beau's stint as a founding partner at Lean Transformations Group (LTG) put him with a group of people who were challenging improvements to the future state mapping methodology that has been captured in *Mapping to See* and *Perfecting Patient Journeys*. Drew began working in earnest to improve the gap in the management system design that never had enough discussions in the value stream mapping literature. And both of us have been working hard to find ways to engage the entire organization in continuous improvement by focusing on the process of socialization. As an added bonus, we've also focused on dropping Japanese terms and a "toolkit focus," replacing this void with helping others learn to think and act differently. It's clearly time to share all we've learned in the past decade!

What a journey, and now here we are back to share with you. The key differences you'll see in this second edition include

- Alignment of value stream improvements to strategic needs
- Incorporation of service examples, including healthcare
- Presentation of future state mapping, which engages conversations and horizontal alignment more quickly
- Deliberate socialization to engage the entire organization in new ways of thinking and acting
- Implementation efforts treated as a learning process through experimentation
- Development of tiered visual management systems to sustain gains and promote continuous improvement

We are excited to share our experiences, our clients' experiences, and our own PDCA learning cycles with you and look forward to seeing how you refashion our learning to meet the needs and culture of your organization.

We hope you enjoy the journey!

Chapter 1

Applying Value Stream Mapping to Information Management

It may surprise some people, but all of the Lean concepts typically applied to manufacturing industries also apply to service organizations as well. The challenge is to be creative enough to figure out how to use them best to align work processes with customers' expectations and make the lives of the staff a bit easier from day to day. In their landmark book *Lean Thinking* (1996), James Womack and Daniel Jones define a value stream as follows:

The set of all specific actions required to bring a specific product or service through the three critical management tasks of any business:

1. Problem solving (e.g., design)
2. Information management (e.g., order processing)
3. Physical transformation (e.g., converting raw materials to finished product)

Management of these value streams—Value Stream Management—involves a process for measuring, understanding, and improving and managing the flow and interactions of all the associated tasks to keep the cost, service, and quality of a company's products and services as competitive as possible. More important, Value Stream Management sets the stage for implementing a Lean transformation throughout the whole enterprise and keeps an organization from falling back into the traditional suboptimal approach of improving departmental-level efficiencies. A basic but powerful two-dimensional tool of Value Stream Management is value stream mapping. It documents and directs a Lean transformation from a system, or big picture, perspective.

Though value stream mapping can identify continued opportunities to enhance value, eliminate waste, and improve flow, it is not the end but the beginning of the journey in Value Stream Management. In W. Edwards Deming's terms, it is the P in the PDCA (*Plan–Do–Check–Act*) improvement cycle (see Figure 1.1). It allows a company to document, measure, and analyze a complex set of relationships as well as

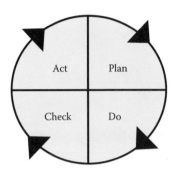

Figure 1.1   **Deming's PDCA improvement cycle.**

BOX 1.1   STEPS FOR SUCCESS IN VALUE STREAM MANAGEMENT

1. Align the strategic direction of the company to the performance of the value stream within the organization.
2. Understand and support the need to improve and manage value streams by engaging the people responsible for the work to redesign the work and improve performance.
3. Align new management processes to support the new work processes.
4. Create Lean metrics that drive and support Lean behavior in creating value, eliminating waste, and monitoring the financial and operating course to strategic success.
5. Implement future-state value stream designs with a focus on scientific experimentation.
6. Demonstrate top-level management's continued leadership in focusing on the organization's pursuit of effective and efficient work methods and management processes throughout the enterprise.

---

to plot a course to create an improved operating strategy and organizational design. Once the company agrees on the design, it is ready to apply the appropriate Lean tools and techniques to improve the performance of the overall value stream. The company manages this value stream by continuing to challenge and redesign its level of cost, quality, and service as perceived by the customers in the markets it serves.

The six steps an organization can use to implement Value Stream Management are highlighted in Box 1.1 and are the focus of this book. Other references on Lean thinking can be found in Appendix I.

Applying Value Stream Mapping to Office and Service Processes

The introduction and application of Lean thinking in the world of office and services has created some confusion, as many companies attempt to emulate the same tools and techniques widely published for the manufacturing environment. We are often approached with these common questions:

- Are there really opportunities to apply the concepts of continuous flow and pull?
- What about mix and volume leveling: Don't these concepts apply only to the manufacturing processes?
- What meaningful Lean metrics can you use to understand and manage the value stream performance?

Clearly, the issue at hand is that many organizations have little experience in applying Lean concepts to nonmanufacturing areas. Further, although a growing number of examples are available for people to learn about applying these concepts, many are still confused about how these examples can translate into their own environments. The intent of this workbook is to provide a basis of understanding as well as the necessary tools to initiate Value Stream Management for the primary work streams that offices and services support. In effect, we are looking at the *information production system.* Our primary focus is to teach the mapping techniques for the information flow and management processes within an enterprise.

In our travels, people have referred to nonmanufacturing as office value streams, service processes, service lines, and a variety of other terms. For the sake of simplicity, we call them value streams (see Figure 1.2). Simply defined, these value streams include all the activities, both those that create value and those that add no value, required to complete a particular service. Examples of value streams include quoting new business, creating a mortgage document, assessing and treating a patient, registering new students in a class, and approving new permits for construction. For readers concerned with the *problem-solving* value stream typically performed by design and development organizations (product, software) these techniques are also directly transferable. We suggest "Value Stream Mapping for Lean Development" (Locher, 2008) as a reference on this subject.

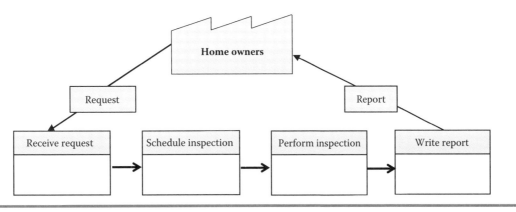

Figure 1.2 Value stream example.

Purpose of the Case Study

In this workbook, we use the case study of the fictional Quick Loan Bank to demonstrate how to use Value Stream Mapping and Management. We will illustrate the step-by-step application of the principles of value stream mapping, including scoping an appropriate redesign effort, mapping the current and future state maps, and implementing the future state. This exercise should give a bird's eye view of Quick Loan Bank's transformation as it goes through the process of improving and managing the work.

It is difficult to cover all possible industries and provide examples for each. We also realize that people often need examples to get started. But please do not look for a solution to your problems in the future state of the case study. Your processes, people, and circumstances are different. We suggest focusing on learning the methodology of value stream mapping a current state and designing a future state based on the key Lean concepts. Once you have a firm grasp of the methodology, you can apply it to any process in any industry.

Chapter 2

Getting Started: Mapping Office and Service Value Streams

Whatever the industry, companies can use the value stream mapping tool to "get their heads and their hands" around even complex processes and systems. They can also use it to develop much needed teamwork across their organizations. The mapping tool is designed to capture the way work is organized and how it progresses throughout an organization (or series of organizations) to enable management to

- Visualize the process from a system perspective
- Point to problems impacting system performance
- Focus the direction of their Lean transformation to a few changes that have great impact on the system

Value stream mapping clearly shows the activities, pathways, and linkages necessary to process information or deliver a service, which, for several reasons, are not always easily identified and understood in office and service environments. First, much information exists and travels in electronic form, which can make it less visible unless methods are put in place to do bring it to the forefront. Next, the sequencing of the activities often varies as information processors or service providers are permitted to do things "their way"—in other words, with little to no standardization. Further, the scheduling of work, the means to trigger the next task or to "link" the activities, is often left unclear. The question, "How do you know when to perform an activity?" gives rise to varied responses, which is particularly concerning given the high-multitasking nature of most office and service environments. To summarize, the flows in office and service environments are loosely structured, which makes it difficult to identify and map their value streams. In addition, information flow is rarely contained in a single department. These circumstances make value stream mapping all the more important. At the same time, however, this context requires greater skill and practice with the tool.

Expanding on the subject of multitasking, it is important to understand that value stream mapping is *not* meant to be applied to a particular department, but rather the information flows that go through that department and, in all likelihood, several others. For example, customer service might be involved in quoting, order entry, invoicing, and marketing activities. Typically, quoting, order entry, and invoicing are all part of the same value stream, but marketing may be a separate activity (and value stream) altogether. Properly defining the value stream to be mapped as part of a preparation or "scoping" activity is critical to success and is covered in this chapter.

The fact is, companies typically view their departments, such as Human Resources, Finance, Engineering, and Purchasing, as organizational "silos" and as independent contributors to the company's success. Because they do not see the interaction and integration of the work activities involving multiple functions and departments, it is no wonder that companies have difficulty grasping the concepts of a new value stream design for office and service.

A company can moderate the inherent challenges of Value Stream Management in the office by identifying and redesigning one or two value streams to begin with, then adding more as it continues its Lean transformation. An identified team will map the activities, the information flow, and the performance of each activity. Next, the team members ask a set of prescriptive questions to challenge the present design of the value stream and draw a new—future—design with enhanced value, better flow, and less waste. As the company continues to address its value streams, it will become easier to see both value and waste and to design more effective value streams and enterprises.

LEAN NOTE

It has been our experience that too often organizations create a current state map, but no true future state. They simply identify all of the waste in the current state and/or "brainstorm" a list of improvement ideas. The result is a *long* "to-do" list that is typically prioritized and assigns people to complete the tasks. However, too often the fundamental way work flows and is performed remains unchanged, and the overall performance of the value stream is unaffected in any *significant* way. Value stream mapping should result in a dramatic improvement in system performance rather than localized, incremental improvement.

As we move forward, you will see how companies can use value stream mapping in their Lean transformation to tackle strategic business issues and organizational challenges: by improving handoffs of work and information; changing information systems; redefining roles and responsibilities of the information processors, service providers, and managers; improving coordination between different offices; and moving or merging activities and even entire organizations. Companies can also extend the use of value stream mapping to include customer and supplier activities. "Macro mapping" entire supply chains can identify other important, even strategic opportunities for improvement.

Understanding Value Stream Mapping Basics

The purpose of value stream mapping is to assist a team in visualizing and communicating not only how its organization acts today, but also how it should act in the future to improve performance in terms of the cost, service, and quality of its products and services. In fact, value stream maps are the essential Lean tools that enable and facilitate value stream management and are the key management tools for continuing to implement and manage new value streams. This is why value stream mapping is the first and most important tool for establishing the direction and focus of a Lean transformation. The following sections provide an overview of how mapping works.

It's about Agreeing!

Although any tool has technical applications, value stream mapping is one of the few Lean tools that also have social implications. In addressing the technical and social components of change in any organization, we've found that the social elements of change are much more dominant in service industries. Value stream mapping is a key social intervention and we approach it as such! In Figure 2.1, you might first notice the technical aspects of the approach, but the verbiage on the right side emphasizes the social aspect: we need to *agree* at each step of the way to ensure that we are all on board with our thinking and actions. A cross-functional value stream has many realities built into the minds of those working within it. Surfacing these realities will allow us to agree on a robust course of action.

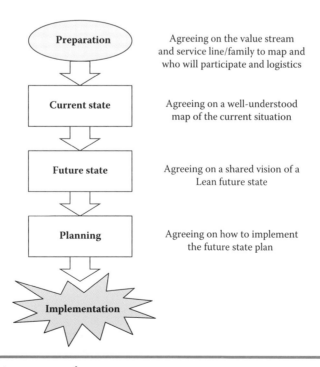

Figure 2.1 Value stream mapping process.

Service Lines

Within a value stream there can be several variations of significance in the service or information being delivered. The steps required can be very dissimilar, or the needs of the customer significantly different based on the specific information or service provided. We call these variations "service lines" (also called service families). Defining a specific service line helps the organization focus its redesign efforts. The identified service line represents all the *related* work and transactions the team seeks to change using the value stream mapping tool. For example, an insurance company might choose "commercial lines," or insurance for businesses, as the value stream to map, and select renewals as the service family to focus on. At a later date the company may choose to map new commercial policies if it sees the need to do so, or perhaps move onto a different value stream such as personal insurance policies. More examples are provided later in this chapter.

Preparation

Picking the right service line to redesign is an important decision. It's best to pick something that is significant to an organization's future, as opposed to one that might be considered "low-hanging fruit." Remember: redesign requires using your human resources. How can these limited resources best serve your organization's needs? To decide where to begin, management typically engages several staff members to consider what is important and determine how much to bite off in the effort, through formal scoping activities. The actual conversations take less than a day to complete, but the effort is completed over a much longer period of time. This allows people to reach out to others for input, to ensure that what they are agreeing to will address the performance issues in their value stream.

Current State

Once the mapping team has agreed on a service line and appropriate scope, it draws a *current state map*. The current state map is the beginning point of the enterprise transformation. It represents how the company organizes and progresses work today; in other words, its baseline condition. The map itself solves no problems. Rather, its purpose is to gather information on a process quickly and visually to point to problems in the company's work streams. Another purpose of mapping the current state is to foster team learning. Team members will understand segments of the current state and how they work, but few to none of them will understand how the *overall* system functions. As they draw the current state map, therefore, team members will learn from each other and develop a common understanding of how the service line really operates. The benefits of the team-building aspect of value stream mapping cannot be overstated. Again and again, we've seen long-standing functional "silos" begin to be removed during a value stream mapping effort. The effort to map the current state should take the team about a day to complete.

Future State

The *future state map* focuses the direction of a new design for the value stream and its intended performance at a specific point in a Lean transformation. Typically, the mapping team's current and future state maps influence each other. That is, many of the team's ideas for the future value stream begin during the current state drawing effort as the team challenges the structure of the current value stream. Likewise, the team often finds the need to collect extra current state information as it designs the future state map. Future states can describe how the value stream should operate over a wide range of timelines. The mapping team might want to draw a picture of how the value stream should operate at the end of three months, or at the end of one year. The timeframe is a critical decision: the longer the timeframe, the more changes the company can incorporate within the future state design. But, if the timeline is too long, organizations can get frustrated waiting for documented change. It's best to keep the first future state design within a three- to six-month timeframe for implementation. This gives a company the ability to complete a few aggressive improvements in a timely manner.

As with the current state map, there is an important social aspect to the design of the future state, as it provides a common vision for how the value steam will function in the future. Everyone will literally be on the same page, which is critical to the successful implementation of the future state. The mapping team should complete the future state map in about a day.

MAPPING TIP

Companies rarely design a future state that requires more than 12 months to implement, as business conditions can change. Therefore, companies must view the future state drawing as an iterative, working document that they can use to drive their continuous improvement efforts.

Planning

The next step is for the mapping team to agree on a detailed work plan for the company to implement. This is designed as a series of specific goals to achieve, along with initial plans to achieve them. Many teams approach the plan development as a series of experiments in work design, visual management, and team engagement. The planning activity is also completed in about a day.

Implementation

The mapping effort is simply a tool: implementing the future state is the key. This is the period of true learning, as up until this time all of the redesign activity is on paper and is filled with hopes and assumptions. The implementation follows the PDCA (*Plan–Do–Check–Act*) cycle: it is merely a plan that can be changed as necessary to achieve the organization's performance goals. Teams are formed during implementation to incorporate tools or thinking to fix the problems they see in formal and informal settings. The changes made should be viewed as experiments that will be performed to see if they have the expected impact. The mapping team identifies these ideas for improvement in the development of the future state map. During implementation, the management team is engaged in changing its management system in support of the new work flows, also with an eye to PDCA with sufficient detail to track, manage, and react to the progress of and learning within the implementation effort. This is often overlooked by organizations and is a common reason for their inability to sustain changes over time.

Getting Started: Scoping the Selected Value Stream and Choosing the Mapping Team

Before the team begins mapping, preparation, or scoping, several activities are necessary to ensure a successful event. The following activities help management set up the company's value stream mapping events.

- Align effort with strategic need and direction.
- Select a value stream.
- Determine a manageable boundary.
- Choose the value stream team.
- Get input from a broad spectrum of colleagues within the identified service line.

We'll discuss each of these next.

Align Effort and Select a Value Stream: Leadership "Catchball" with the Redesign Teams

Whether the mandate of the company is to redesign an entire value stream or a specific set of related functions or activities within the organization, the leadership team must first define the linkage between the company's strategic objectives and the performance it needs to achieve to make those goals. This is typically done in a session with organizational leaders, who are tasked with answering the following questions:

- What are the key elements of your strategic objectives over the next one to three years?
- Where does your performance need to be?
- What value streams and service lines within the selected value streams are you most concerned about to meet the needs of your company's overall business strategy?

■ What shortfalls exist in the selected value stream that create risk for the organization? What is the impact of these shortfalls to both the customers and the people working within the value stream?

■ What are the specific performance targets for the value stream in measurable terms (e.g., service, quality, cost, staff satisfaction, etc.)?

Examples of the output from the discussion might be the following:

■ Local government permit application takes too long, leading to businesses moving to another locale. Target performance is two weeks for permits.

■ Call center response time leads to unhappy customers and the risk of losing market share. Target performance is all complaints resolved within ten minutes.

■ Home Health referrals for hospital inpatients are dropping, leading to an increase in hospital readmissions. Target performance is a 50% reduction in hospital readmissions.

■ Receivables are increasing and preventing us from investing in future needs. Target performance is a 50% decrease in outstanding days.

Once leadership agrees on the problems to address and the performance targets that must be met, this information is then communicated to a cross-functional team(s) representing the identified value stream. This is commonly known as "catchball," where different levels and functions of an organization align activities with the company's strategic objectives. In this case, once leadership communicates the initial needs, the identified team "catches" this information and aligns it with what the team members know of the value stream and its problems from their (closer) perspective.

Determine a Manageable Boundary

The cross-functional team typically meets to discuss the value stream that leadership selected and the targets identified in more detail from its own perspectives. The meeting involves discussing the following points:

1. *How much (and what portion) of the value stream needs to be addressed to meet the performance needs?* The team may believe that addressing only a portion of the value stream would provide the necessary improvement in performance. Referring to the examples previously provided, this might be
   – Only the environmental permit process
   – The call center's responses from initial call to the end of the last call necessary to resolve the issue
   – Patient care activities beginning at morning rounds and continuing through the first shift
   – The front end efforts resulting in the initial customer invoice

2. *Do we need to address all the work in the value stream, or should we focus on a specific service line?* The team will need to understand that not all work is the same within the value stream, and that agreeing on what type of work is in and out of bounds can help clarify the focus. Using the previous examples, possible service lines include
   - Excluding environmental permits for companies that renew, but including permits for "first timers"
   - Excluding specific types of customer service requests such as those that are technical in nature, but including all others (e.g., order status, product availability)
   - Excluding young or healthy patients but including anyone who has had at least one readmission in the last two years
   - Excluding a specific type of invoicing, such as international invoices

---

MAPPING TIP

Clearly defining the boundaries is very important to a successful mapping effort. It will help keep the team focused throughout the process and avoid distractions, or getting off track altogether. It has been our experience that periodic review of the project boundaries and scope during the event help to avoid what is often referred to as "scope creep," where the scope of the project expands beyond what was originally intended.

---

3. *Who needs to be represented in the redesign?* Once the leadership team has agreed on the first two points, making sure that all parties who work in or support this scope are involved is critical to both the technical and social needs of change. This initial list can represent any combination of functions and specific people.
4. *Who needs to lead the redesign effort?* This is a critical role that we refer to as a "value stream manager." The value stream manager is often the person who presently oversees the largest portion of the value stream. To recall, most value streams flow through multiple departments or functions. Often, there is no single person identified to manage and improve a particular value stream. Few companies have organized themselves by value stream. Therefore, identifying this person is not always straightforward, but absolutely necessary for success for reasons we will discuss shortly.
5. *What are the basic work steps that occur within the boundary we've agreed to?* It's a good idea to confirm the boundaries and in/out-of-scope thoughts by sketching out a high-level representation of the basic process that will be redesigned. This is a good way to confirm that the scoping team has a common understanding of the effort intended and will lead to discussions about the right people to have on the team based on the work steps.

Choose the Value Stream Team

The team designing the new value stream should be made up of those people who work inside the functions that support the value stream under study. Ample time must be given for team members to be educated in Lean thinking and value stream mapping. The best scenario would be to have the team involved in the key preparation activities discussed in this chapter. The team should consist of a value stream manager and supporting cross-functional team members. These are described in the following sections.

Value Stream Manager

The value stream manager is the person assigned to lead the future state design implementation across functional and departmental boundaries. This person can also be responsible for the ongoing success of value stream management.

The value stream manager must be knowledgeable, respected within the organization, and have good facilitating and coaching skills. It is imperative that management not only select a qualified value stream manager, but also create the appropriate work environment for the selected person to perform in. A frequent problem is that management assigns an employee to be a part-time value stream manager, while his or her "regular" job still reports to the department head of the very department being redesigned. This creates a potential for the department head to assert his or her command and control and trump any changes the value stream manager is trying to oversee. To avoid this conflict of interest, management must select the person for this role carefully and provide the value stream manager with the political support necessary for the difficult tasks required to enable change. Organizations may want to consider a change in reporting relationships to give the value stream manager the resources and authority necessary to implement the future state successfully and practice continuous improvement over time.

LEAN NOTE

Ask yourself this question: "Looking ahead, who will be responsible for the *continuous* improvement of the redesigned value stream?" The real objective of Lean is to practice continuous improvement. In other words, the effort should not end after implementation of the first future state. The value stream to be addressed is of great importance to the organization and to meeting its strategic objectives. Shouldn't we continue the effort beyond the first significant cycle of improvement? If so, who will keep the organization focused on its continuous improvement over time? These are important questions indeed, and hopefully will get readers to consider more deeply the role of value stream manger.

Cross-Functional Team Members

The value stream team members are responsible for completing the value stream analysis, which includes current and future state mapping and assisting the value stream manager in implementing the new value stream design. Depending on the scope, management needs to select a cross-functional team with representatives from each of the primary functional areas impacted by the selected value stream. In total, six to eight members may be directly involved in the actual mapping events, and other members may be involved on an as-needed basis.

When identifying prospective team members, consider the position that he or she holds in the organization's hierarchy as well as his or her attitude. While knowledge of the work and how it is performed is important to the successful completion of the current state map, so is the ability to challenge today's practices to create a future state that will meet the defined objectives. People in supervisor or manager roles can learn how the value stream currently functions through direct observation of or discussion with associates who regularly perform the work. This can be accomplished before or even during the mapping event. However, some associates might not be comfortable challenging current practices in significant ways, preferring to defer to management. The willingness to consider alternatives to "business as usual" must be a characteristic of team members regardless of title.

Capture the Scoping Thoughts and Agreements on an SIPOC Diagram

A good way to capture thoughts to share the team's thinking is something we've borrowed from the Six Sigma community: a modified SIPOC (Supplier–Input–Process–Output–Customer) diagram. All of the elements of the scoping discussion can be found in the example provided in Figure 2.2.

Get Input from a Broad Spectrum of Colleagues within the Identified Service Line

This can be described as horizontal catchball to engage others in the organization and their perspectives. While the cross-functional scoping effort will represent some good thinking, there are as many opinions about what should be studied as there are people working within the value stream and selected service line! The social aspects of value stream redesign are attended to by the team, who will share their scoping thoughts and actively seek other points of view to make sure they head down a clear path for the redesign work. We've typically seen that the more that is invested in this scoping activity, the better the alignment of the organization. The core communication document is the SIPOC diagram, which tells a story for others to think through, discuss, challenge, and modify on the way to alignment. At the end of the catchball, the SIPOC will be finalized and then shared with the leadership team to ensure that the agreed on

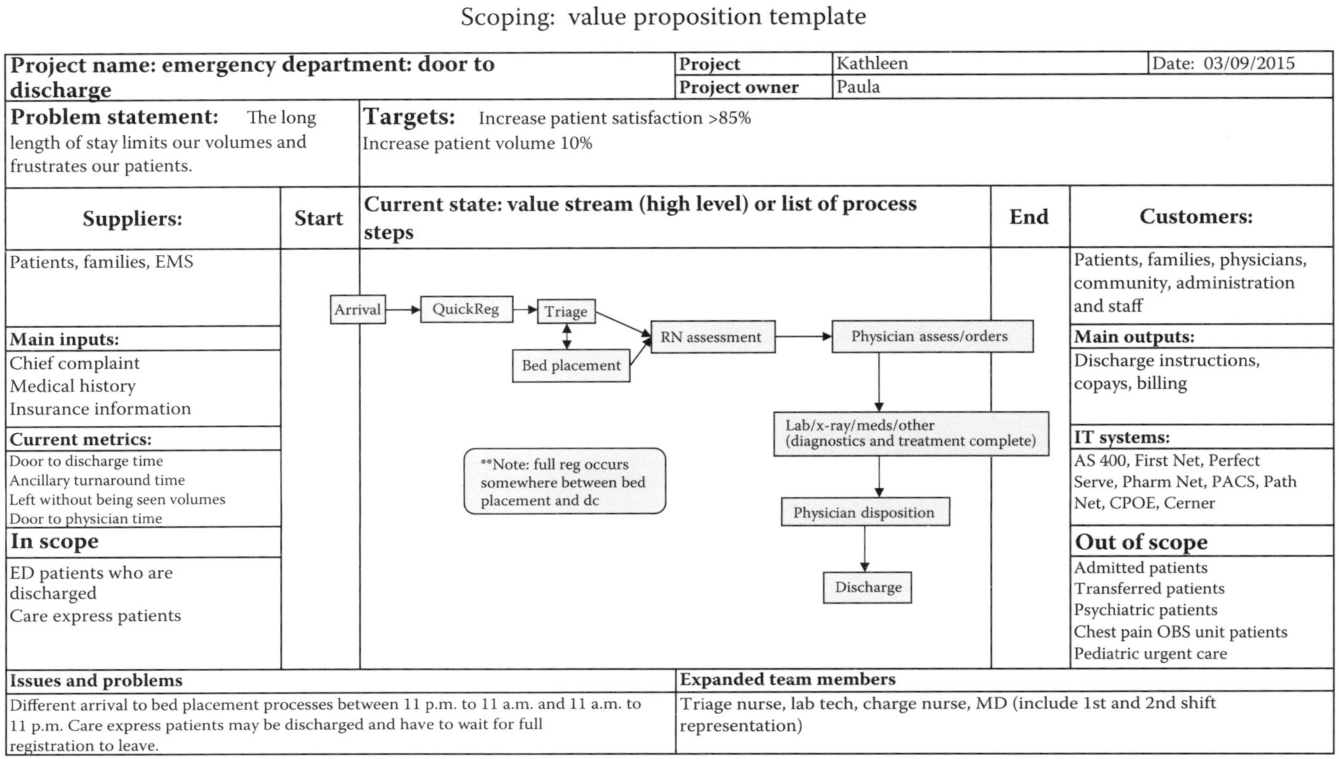

Scoping: value proposition template

Project name: emergency department: door to discharge		Project	Kathleen	Date: 03/09/2015
		Project owner	Paula	

Problem statement: The long length of stay limits our volumes and frustrates our patients.

Targets: Increase patient satisfaction >85%
Increase patient volume 10%

Suppliers:	Start	Current state: value stream (high level) or list of process steps	End	Customers:
Patients, families, EMS		Arrival → QuickReg → Triage ↔ Bed placement → RN assessment → Physician assess/orders → Lab/x-ray/meds/other (diagnostics and treatment complete) → Physician disposition → Discharge **Note: full reg occurs somewhere between bed placement and dc		Patients, families, physicians, community, administration and staff
Main inputs: Chief complaint Medical history Insurance information				**Main outputs:** Discharge instructions, copays, billing
Current metrics: Door to discharge time Ancillary turnaround time Left without being seen volumes Door to physician time				**IT systems:** AS 400, First Net, Perfect Serve, Pharm Net, PACS, Path Net, CPOE, Cerner
In scope				**Out of scope**
ED patients who are discharged Care express patients				Admitted patients Transferred patients Psychiatric patients Chest pain OBS unit patients Pediatric urgent care

Issues and problems

Different arrival to bed placement processes between 11 p.m. to 11 a.m. and 11 a.m. to 11 p.m. Care express patients may be discharged and have to wait for full registration to leave.

Expanded team members

Triage nurse, lab tech, charge nurse, MD (include 1st and 2nd shift representation)

Figure 2.2 SIPOC example.

activities will meet the needs of the organization in the eyes of the leaders. The team will also find it helpful to review the SIPOC periodically while mapping, as well as during implementation. Continued alignment of the team's efforts to the defined direction is important. This is invaluable in avoiding the previously mentioned "scope creep," where a team begins drifting toward an unintended direction.

Once the team is established, the members must gain an understanding of some of the specific kinds of waste that occur in their work. We'll talk about these in the next chapter.

Chapter 3

Identifying Office and Service Waste

The identification and elimination of waste from all work processes is a key concept of Lean thinking. However, there are some challenges to seeing waste in office and service environments. Often waste is created and then disappears in very short timeframes, and doesn't always leave physical evidence of its existence. In other words, it tends to be less tangible. For example, a service quality issue might be resolved relatively quickly, giving people the impression that there is little or no defect or correction waste. We have learned, though, that it takes much practice to develop "eyes for waste." Value stream mapping, with its icons and data, will help greatly here, as we'll show in subsequent chapters.

Eliminating waste can also be challenging. There is a strong tendency to explain it away, with people making the case that the waste in question is necessary or "business required." It is true that all waste cannot be eliminated, but that should not deter you from trying. Even when it can't be eliminated, waste can often be reduced. Identifying the root causes of the waste and addressing those that impede the organization's ability to meet its objectives is a fundamental skill required of all Lean practitioners.

This is why it is important that the organization, as well as the value-stream team members, have or develop a working knowledge of Lean principles to complement this workbook. There are many excellent books to educate the workforce, such as *Lean Thinking* (Womack and Jones, 1996), *Lean Office and Service Simplified* (Locher, 2011), and *Lean Lexicon* (edited by Chet Marchwinski and John Shook, 2013).

Determining Value from Waste in Office and Service Activities

In processing information or delivering a service, three categories of value streams exist based on whether they

1. Create value as perceived by the customer
2. Create no value for the customer but are currently required to support the various needs of the business
3. Create no value as perceived by the customer or the business

Many of the activities that take place in an office and service environment are in the second group, and include support departments such as human resources, accounting, risk management, and so forth. Although the customer may not care about these activities, the company can't survive without them—although there may be non-value-added work within these incidental functions. Because these actions are required to support the existing business model, the company cannot eliminate them until it reconsiders its existing business model. When a company travels the path to become a Lean enterprise, it must challenge the entire business model. Otherwise, the actions in the second group will remain unchanged, and the company may not be able to attain its business strategy and objectives.

This is why one of the first orders of business for the team members in understanding the office value stream is to be able to distinguish value from waste. Office and service wastes abound, and some simple examples to stimulate the thought processes of the team members listed as

1. Overproduction: Producing more information or service than is needed and/or sooner than is needed by the customer. Examples: Overly detailed reports, highly detailed planning processes, financial planning too far into the future
2. Inventory: Anything that is in excess of one-piece flow, or batch processing. Examples: Processing invoices once per week, completing all performance evaluations at the same time of the year
3. Correction: Any activity that is performed to correct an error that has been made. Examples: Correcting order entry errors, issuing credits due to invoice errors, hiring an unqualified person for a position
4. Extra processing: Steps that take longer than they should, or entire activities that do not add value for the customer. Examples: A company's budgeting process (adds no value to the external customer and questionable value to internal customers), meetings that take longer to conduct than they should, requiring excessive approvals, asking a patient the same question multiple times
5. Motion: Movement of office and service personnel. Examples: Walking to and from centralized files, printers, the facsimile machine, and so on; nurses running for supplies, medications, or equipment that is needed
6. Transportation: Movement of information or materials. Examples: e-mail, handing off paperwork or customers to another person

7. Waiting: Customers or information waiting to be serviced or worked on. Examples: Waiting on decisions to be made, problems to be resolved, system response time, and so forth
8. Underutilized people: Not using people's full skills and abilities. Examples: Affording people only narrow responsibilities, insufficient cross training, overly limited authority

Learning to distinguish between value and waste begins with recognizing many of the activities that are performed every day in a business for what they really are–waste that adds cost to the business, but no value to the customer. While some readers may be familiar with the traditional seven wastes, we have added an eighth, "underutilized people," to reflect waste created by not using a person's full mental, creative, and physical abilities. Some of the examples in the list above may surprise you.

TEAM EXERCISE

As a team orientation exercise, identify office and service waste that currently exists in the value stream and/or service line to be studied. Then apply the "five whys" technique. For each example of waste, ask the question "why" several times whenever the team identifies a reason for the waste. Repeatedly asking the question "why" leads the team to identifying its root cause, and consequently often to many surprises, questions, and discussions.

When companies do address waste in an office and service environment, the initial reaction of many is to address *all* forms of waste all at once. In fact, we have encountered many organizations that take a brainstorming approach to the development of the future state for whatever business process they are working to improve. They identify *all* wastes in the current state and generate ideas to address them all. This scattershot approach is time consuming, resource consuming, and generally ineffective in its application.

A more effective approach is to revisit the direction and objectives of the organization and the process that is the subject of the value stream map. Next, the team should identify those wastes that are truly impeding the ability of the process to meet those objectives. It is about selecting a few key wastes rather than all of the current ones: "quality, not quantity," as the saying goes. Further, this should be done in the context of a comprehensive process redesign that can be accomplished only by applying the future state questions covered later in the book.

As we've mentioned, value stream mapping requires data, which is one of the aspects that sets it apart from traditional process mapping. Much of the data will help the team to highlight waste. For most organizations, the cost, service, and quality of many office and service activities are unknown. Therefore, it is common for the team to struggle when mapping a particular business process for the first time. We will discuss the subject of office and service metrics in Chapter 5, and provide some tips to help with that process.

In the next chapter we introduce the Quick Loan Bank case study. We will provide an overview of the company's business case, and see how the company used value stream mapping as a tool and Lean as a strategy to improve the performance of its processing of loans.

Chapter 4

Introduction to the Quick Loan Bank Case Study

Quick Loan Bank provides banking services to businesses and consumers, including loans of various types. It has identified auto loans as a service with significant growth potential. The bank would like to begin its effort in this area by focusing on used car auto loans, which represent a high level of activity in their region. These loans are typically set up by the car dealers, without much effort on the consumer's part. These auto dealers shop for the best terms on loans when selling cars to consumers. In addition, they are also concerned with turnaround time of terms, approvals, and paperwork, as they would like to close a deal while the customer is still on the lot. Senior management of the bank felt that Lean management's strong customer focus and emphasis on flow would help them achieve their goal of increased market share by simplifying the process and significantly reducing turnaround time.

Currently, their loan win rate averages only 8.5% of the total number of loan applications received from dealers. Quick Loan Bank would like to improve this figure to 17% within the next year. Senior management has received complaints from its customers about its turnaround time, which has been identified as the primary reason that Quick Loan Bank loses business to its competitors. The bank needs to find a way to reduce the turnaround time, ideally with existing resources. A cross-functional management team is meeting to plan and scope the project. It will then hand this off to a team closer to the work to map the value stream and to determine how best to meet the defined goals.

Scoping

The cross-functional management team performed a quick walk-through of the existing process to improve their understanding of it. Used car auto loan applications are submitted by dealers to one of three Quick Loan Bank's loan centers. Time and effort are expended in reviewing and responding to these applications, but more than 90% of them do not result in successful loans. The management team agreed to focus on one loan center for the purposes of the value stream mapping exercise, believing that what they learn at one center can be applied to the other two.

The management team decided that the vice president of Auto Loans will be the value stream manager, as she is already responsible for this part of the Quick Loan Bank business. The Leadership Team will be made up of the bank president and the VP of Lending, who, at the appropriate time, will review the team's proposals, provide guidance, and ensure alignment to business needs. The management team's understanding of the value stream, gained by the actual walk-through, made it easy for them to identify who needs to be on the value stream mapping team. Team members will include the supervisor of the used car auto loans, two underwriters, two loan processors, and two buyers, along with two dealers, who will bring a valuable customer perspective throughout the project. There are a total of nine team members; other members of the organization may be called on to participate on an as-needed basis.

Next, the management team identified the key customers and suppliers of the value stream: obviously car dealers and consumers in this case. Suppliers include the dealers and consumers as well, as they provide important information for the value stream. In addition, employers provide proof of employment and insurance companies provide proof of insurance—both important pieces of information required in the value stream. As previously mentioned, two dealers will be on the team. Again, other suppliers and/or customers can be contacted as the need arises.

The mapping event will be scheduled over several days in December. This will provide sufficient time for the members of the value mapping team to receive training on Lean management and value stream mapping before they map the actual process, as well as to perform a thorough walk-through of the process, similar to the one already performed by the cross-functional management team. The management team felt strongly that such education and "going to see" will be important to the success of the event. In addition, there will be enough time for the team to share what it has learned at key points of the mapping process, including the first drafts of the current and future state maps. Training will be provided on December 4, and the team will begin to create the current state map on the same day. Completion of the current state map is targeted for December 5. The team will then share the map and their reflections of the current state with the appropriate staff members during a report-out, scheduled toward the end of the day on the 5th. At that time the team will schedule another day to create the future state map. The time in between will be used to share the current state with others who are involved in the value stream to confirm the validity of the map and to gather their thoughts. Similar report-out and sharing activities will be conducted for the future state once its mapping has been completed. The management team felt strongly that these socialization activities will be key to a successful effort.

Some data will be collected prior to the mapping event, such as the volume data summarized in Figure 4.1. The rest will be gathered by the mapping team during the value stream mapping event itself. This includes the process and lead time for each process step, as well as a measure of the information quality as received by each step.

A review of the volume of used car auto loans by day of the week reveals what many had suspected. More than 50% of the volume occurs on just two days of the week: Mondays and Saturdays. This will be valuable information for the value stream mapping team as they seek to understand how things work today, in the current state, as well as when they consider changes in the future.

The information collected by the management team during the scoping exercise was summarized in a SIPOC document. To recall, SIPOC is an acronym for *Suppliers–Inputs–Processes–Outputs–Customers*. The draft SIPOC was then reviewed with staff at the other locations to receive their input. The revised SIPOC is shown in Figure 4.2. It will be reviewed with the value stream mapping team at the start of the effort, and will be an important reference throughout the project. Periodic review of the goals and objectives, as well as what falls in scope and out of scope will keep the team focused as it moves forward.

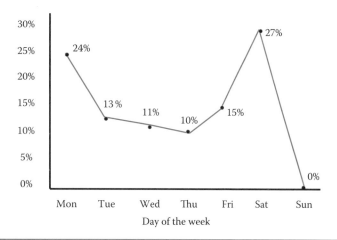

Figure 4.1   Volume of used car auto loan applications, percent by day.

Used Car Auto Loan Project

Project name: Used Car Auto Loan Process
Value stream owner: VP Auto Loans
Leadership team: Bank President, VP of Lending

Service family: Applications through Central Loan Center

Workshop dates: December 4–6, 2014, 9:00 AM–5:00 PM, Lunch noon–1:00, Report out 12/6, 4–5:00

Workshop location: Loan Center 'A'

Objectives:
Increase market share
Reduce turnaround time for loan/loan approval
Goals:
Increase win rate to 15% with no increase in employment

Suppliers:
Dealers
Consumers
Insurance companies
Employers

Inputs:
Contract information
Loan requests
Employment and personal informaton
Employment verification
Credit verification

Start:
Dealer sends loan request

End:
Loan scanned

Key process boxes:
Review loan application
Review loan, set pricing and terms
Communicate terms to dealer
Negotiate loan
Receive contract from dealer
Verify contract package
Contact references (employers, insurance companies, etc.)
Process exceptions
Fund loan
Scan loan documentation

Outputs:
Loan information
Requests for information
Loan terms

Customers:
Loan servicing group
Employers
Insurance companies
Car dealers

Issues/problems:
Low capture rate
High demand variation
Uneven work balance
Too many handoffs
Long lead times
Poor loan information quality
Many exceptions prior to funding

Benefits:
Happier dealers
More business
Better work balance
Higher leveraged workforce

In scope:
All types of consumers
Used car dealers

Out of scope:
Loan production offices
New car dealers

Technology:
BankLoans
LoRisk

Participants:
Dealers (2)
Underwriters
Loan processors
Buyers
Supervisor

Data to collect:
% C&A
Process time
Lead time
Yield
Position involved
Demand by day

Figure 4.2 SIPOC for Quick Loan Bank used car auto loan process.

Chapter 5

Assessing the Current State

As discussed, the current state map documents how a company is currently doing business and is the basis for designing a future state and initiating true Value Stream Management. To begin creating the current state map, the mapping team needs to understand not only the logistics of drawing the map, but also what metrics to select to measure the effectiveness of the value stream in terms of cost, service, and quality. For the purpose of this workbook, we chose seven steps to help the team in both of these areas (see Box 5.1). In this chapter, we concentrate mostly on Step 3, selecting process metrics. In Chapter 6, we will apply all seven steps to the Quick Loan Bank case study. As the mapping team moves forward, these steps should be used as a guideline to create a current state map.

BOX 5.1   SUGGESTED STEPS TO COMPLETE A CURRENT STATE MAP

1. Document customer information and needs.
2. Identify the main processes (in order).
3. Select process metrics.
4. Perform value stream walk-through and fill in data boxes, including queues and resident technology.
5. Establish how each process prioritizes work.
6. Calculate system summary metrics, such as total lead time, total process time, percent complete and accurate, cost, and/or other value stream summary measures.
7. Consider this a draft document until you socialize it with the others working in the value stream.

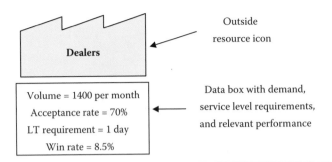

Figure 5.1 Depicting customer-related data.

Step 1: Document Customer Information and Needs

Having a strong customer focus is critical to Lean thinking. Therefore, it should come as no surprise that we begin here. When creating the customer information and needs document, the team should first use the outside resource icon to represent the customer or customers (see Figure 5.1; the data shown are from the Quick Loan Bank case study). Next, a data box to define customer needs should be added below the outside resource icon. These can include demand or frequency that the value stream is performed, service level requirements, and quality expectations. If demand varies, consider expressing the demand in a range. It is important for the team to understand the amount of variation within the current situation. In addition, consider including measures in the data box indicating how well the current process is meeting these requirements. Customer satisfaction ratings, number of complaints in a period, and the percentage of time that service levels are met are just a few examples.

Step 2: Identify the Main Processes (in Order)

It is important that *processes*, not departments or functions, be identified in the process box. The focus is on the activities required to process information, not on titles or names of people. Sometimes, it might be helpful to note the department currently performing the task. The team can note this in a process box if necessary (see Figure 5.2). The team will usually perform this step as a group in the classroom or conference room and make any necessary changes as they walk the process (Step 4).

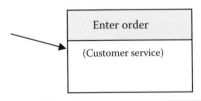

Figure 5.2 Process box icon with note of department or function performing it.

During this step, a decision must be made regarding the level of detail desired. In other words, how many process boxes should we have? When should one process box end and the next one begin? There are several guidelines to consider, the most important of which is time, specifically lead time. To recall, we use value stream mapping to create "eyes for waste," and we can also add "eyes for flow." We want to identify points in the value stream where flow stops and queue begins. However, we do not want to highlight every stoppage of flow, just the significant ones. What makes one stoppage significant when another is not? The answer comes by comparing the typical length of time of the stoppage to the overall lead time for the value stream. If the overall lead time is 200 days, we certainly should not concern ourselves with stoppages of minutes or hours. If there is a queue between two process steps, but it is insignificant, then you should consider combining the boxes.

An easy guideline to follow is to have a different process box every time there is a handoff from one person to another. In our experience, significant stoppages often occur at these points and therefore should be highlighted. In other words, process boxes represent the work between handoffs, but the stoppages that occur before a handoff can also best be displayed within the process box. (An example is provided later in this chapter.)

The same discussion can take place with process time—the time that it takes to perform particular processes. If the current process involves 400 people-hours, we probably should not concern ourselves with processes that require several minutes to complete. We may want to consider combining quickly performed processes with other boxes, along with appropriate notes to avoid confusion.

MAPPING TIP

Always consider the total lead time and total process time for the current value stream when determining the appropriate level of detail for the current state map. Focus on the processes that are significant contributors to both. Excessive detail does not necessarily provide important new knowledge when assessing the current state. Too much detail can really sidetrack a team from the agreed-on scope of the mapping event. As a general guideline, try to keep the overall number of process boxes between 7 and 12: this "altitude" will keep you from getting into the weeds while providing enough detail to see systemic problems.

Step 3: Select Process Metrics

Selecting metrics for current state maps can be troublesome because many office and service processes have no standard performance metrics reflecting cost, service, and quality within the value stream. The process metrics that follow are a good starting point for the team. The team may find that several of these metrics are unique to the organization, or they might select other metrics to support their

BOX 5.2   PROCESS METRICS

1. Time: Process time, lead time
2. Percent complete and accurate
3. Number of iterations
4. Typical batch sizes or practices
5. Demand rate
6. Number of people
7. Queues
8. Information technology used

visualization of the process and the inherent problems in the value stream. Of course, not all metrics apply to every process.

It is important to understand how the data will be used to analyze the current state and in designing a future state. As always, we want to highlight waste. The discussion that took place in Chapter 3, "Identifying Office and Service Waste," should help us to select process metrics that will do just that. But there is more to consider, which we discuss as we review each metric. Keep in mind that each metric may not apply to every process box.

We will also need to understand how the data will be obtained from the existing value stream. Although it is ideal to obtain these data first hand through observation, this may not always be possible during the mapping event. Perhaps these data can be collected by team members *prior* to the event through direct observation? If not, maybe the data can be obtained from historic records. Short of that, we have used people's "best guesses." At the high "altitude" level that value stream mapping usually represents, "best-guess" estimates usually work just fine (Box 5.2).

MAPPING NOTE

We are discussing these metrics to suggest possible ways to measure a company's process(es). Don't use all of them! Select a few that make sense and get started with a map to see what you learn. You may need to include some that are useful for exposing problems discussed during the scoping session: What's holding you back and how can you measure it? But, we typically include process time, lead time, and percent complete and accurate in each map.

Time

There are several definitions of time. We offer two common definitions the team can use when discussing the important subject of time.

Process Time

This is the actual time it takes to complete a process or activity. The team can usually quantify process time by observation. For example, it takes five minutes to enter an order from beginning to end, uninterrupted. Process times may vary for a number of reasons (e.g., worker capability, customer type, order type, etc.). When this happens, the team needs to determine whether these variations represent out-of-scope conditions, or if some other explanation exists. The data could then be displayed in a range (e.g., 5 to 10 minutes per order) with a note about why the variation occurs. Be specific with unit of measure (e.g., per order, per line item). The exact meaning of the data on the map should be clear to everyone.

Lead Time

This is the elapsed time associated with completing an activity. It is measured from the time the activity enters someone's inbox to the time it leaves the desk complete (normally to the next inbox.). Lead time is generally greater than process time, as work can sit in a queue waiting for someone either to begin the process or to complete it following interruptions. For example, it may take just five minutes to enter an order (i.e., process time). However, questions might arise, leading the person to put the order aside for a period of time. Therefore, the five-minute order entry task may actually take two hours to complete (i.e., lead time) while the person is waiting for answers. The team can also note reasons for excessive lead time, such as order errors or multiple interruptions. If possible, distinguish between the lead time in queue from the lead time due to the stop-and-start scenario just described. Both can be displayed on the map, as shown in Figure 5.3.

LEAN NOTE

If a person practices true one-piece flow, or process-one–move-one, without interruption, then process time equals lead time. An example of this is seen when an order is processed and handed to the next person in the value stream, who then immediately begins to process the information.

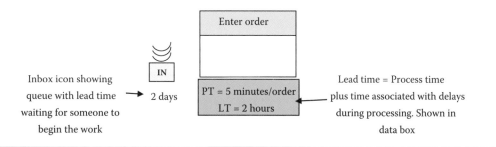

Figure 5.3 Depicting lead time and process time.

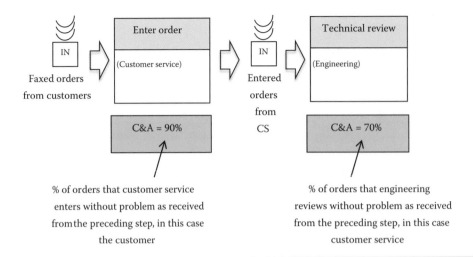

Figure 5.4 Determining and displaying percent complete and accurate.

Percent Complete and Accurate

Percent Complete and Accurate (% C&A) is a process quality metric used to describe how often an activity *receives* information that is complete and accurate from the perspective of the recipient. Paperwork or other transactions might not contain necessary information, or might be confusing or illegible. The % C&A attribute is one way to quantify the inability of the process to meet the internal customer requirements within the value stream, which typically results in extending both the process time and lead time to support the value stream.

For instance, if an order is faxed to Customer Service, the staff might review the order for legibility, ship-to information, and so forth. The percentage of orders Customer Service enters without a problem is the % C&A. Extending this example, if Engineering then reviews the entered order it might find some technical information missing from the order. In this case, Engineering might have a different % C&A baseline, as it has a different perspective on an order requirement. It is for this reason that we always ask the *recipient* the question concerning % C&A. Collecting this information prior to the mapping event can really help; it is noted in the data box for the corresponding process box as shown in Figure 5.4.

Number of Iterations

This can be an important data attribute in some office and service processes. It can take several attempts or iterations to complete an activity, often due to a lack of information from a prior process (i.e., a % C&A less than 100%), or errors created and discovered within a process. The iteration icon can be used to highlight the points in the process where this occurs, as well as the possible impact on lead time and/or process time, and in a simple way that does not add unnecessary complexity to the map. This is shown in Figure 5.5.

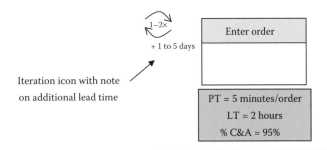

Figure 5.5 Depicting iteration icon.

Typical Batch Sizes or Practices

Typical batch size or batching practices represent how much or how often work is performed. For many office functions, there is a certain routine in place. For example, the accounting function in a small company might follow this timetable:

- Mondays: Invoices.
- Tuesdays: Payables.
- Wednesdays: General Ledger.
- Thursdays: Payroll.
- Fridays: Reports.

In this example, every activity is performed once per week, creating a batch size of one week. For paperwork (e.g., invoices) waiting in a batch as long as one week, the lead time could be as high as one week. So, this batch size can be related to lead time, and in this case, it may make sense to use batch size in place of the traditional lead time. Often, batch practices are associated with overnight processing of data by an organization's computerized information systems.

Demand Rate

Demand rate represents the volume of transactions seen at each process over a specified period, such as orders per day, line items per order, and so forth. This is a key attribute, as it explicitly states a customer requirement. The team uses this to design a system capable of responding to customer requirements. If applicable, the team should also note the range of demand along with a note explaining the variation. For example, one company we worked with completed 80% of its invoicing in the last week of each month.

The demand rate unit of measure will change based on the nature of the activity. For example, the number of orders received per day may be an appropriate measure of demand on an order processing activity in one organization. In other companies, a more appropriate measure will be the number of line items. The number of shipped orders per day may be an appropriate measure of demand on an invoicing process, as the number of line items in an order may be irrelevant to the invoicing process.

Number of People

The number of people metric can represent one of two situations. The first is simply the number of people trained to do or responsible for doing the work. For instance, there could be four people capable of entering orders, even though only one person physically enters them at any point in time. This representation shows how widespread the task knowledge is, identifying issues of cross-training, or the lack thereof. A good question to ask is: "Is this the only person who knows how to perform this activity?" Cross-training is often lacking in office and service processes because many activities can be put on hold until the one person who knows how to perform the activity can get to it.

The second way to use the number of people metric is to represent the number of full-time equivalents (sometimes referred to as FTEs) who regularly perform each business process. When used with process time, the number of people can be compared with the demand rate to verify the capacity of each business process. For example, if a transaction takes 30 minutes to complete at a certain step and the value stream has a demand of 20 transactions per day, then a capacity of 600 minutes per day is necessary to support the value stream at that step.

Estimating the number of people and the percentage of time that they typically spend on a specific task can be difficult in an office environment. Office personnel often perform multiple tasks and are unaware of the time they spending on individual ones. This is another piece of information that the team will want to have people track prior to the mapping event. Sometimes, their best guess is sufficient for our purposes here. For example, five people might estimate that they spend approximately 20% of their time performing a specific process. Here, you can depict the percentage with a simple formula (see Figure 5.6). In this example, we can easily determine that there is one full-time equivalent person currently performing this task.

MAPPING TIP

The number of people and percentage of time that they spend on a specific process may or may not be required on every value stream map. It will depend on the objectives defined for the event. For example, if increasing capacity is important to meet an expected increase in future demand, then these data will be more relevant. If it is deemed important, then we offer the following suggestion. For various reasons it may be difficult to overcome people's reluctance to estimate the percentage of time they spend on a task. At times, it may be necessary for the team to collect this information over time—say one week—to firm up the estimate. Then they can revise the data on the current state map, if necessary. In this way, the team can easily overcome a difficult obstacle to the mapping process while getting the necessary information.

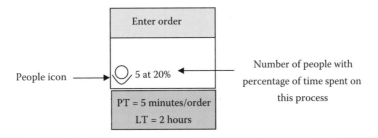

Figure 5.6 Number of people and percent of time.

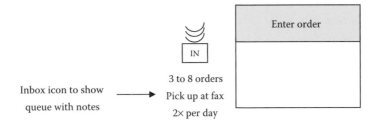

Figure 5.7 Inbox icon.

Queues

Queues can take many forms in office and service processes, for example, queues of information or queues of customers. Most often, queues are symptoms of a lack of flow. In information flows the queues typically reside as paperwork or electronic files. The unit of measure can vary based on the nature of the business process. Examples include

- Orders queued at the fax machine or in an online system
- Various forms in people's inboxes
- Work stored in e-mails (e.g., messages, requests for information, files)
- Design projects in queue or underway
- Line items awaiting purchasing to process, and so on
- People waiting in phone queues or in line at a store

In Figure 5.3 we introduced the inbox icon that is used to depict queues. We show it again in Figure 5.7, with notes explaining the nature of the piles of paperwork or electronic queues of information that can arise in a value stream. Queues are normally associated with batch processing and long lead times. They can also be indicators of bottlenecks or constraints in the value stream. Queues can vary based on the time of day/week/month, so they need to be expressed as a range with a note describing the nature of the variation.

Information Technology Used

Information technology used describes the tools used to assist the processing of the information at each process box, or the sources of information needed to

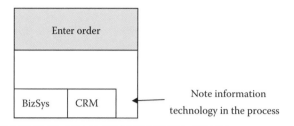

Figure 5.8 **Displaying information technology used.**

perform a process. Most often it refers to software tools, databases, and the like. The team records these in a lower corner of the process box (see Figure 5.8). There may be several technologies used within a process box, and several others used in different process boxes. This apparent lack of integration can be a root cause for long lead times, lack of flow, extra processing, and quality-related problems.

Keys to Selecting Process Metrics

The purpose of value stream metrics is to help the team visualize a process and identify process issues. The metrics we've discussed are helpful in most cases, but aren't intended to represent every situation. There may be specific issues to visualize in a particular company's value streams that require some creative metrics or icons to "tell the story." Here are some key points to remember when selecting metrics.

- The information the team collects in the documentation of the current state map is for identifying the cost, service, and quality performance of the various elements of the value stream.
- In many cases, the team uses the collected documentation to highlight areas of value, waste, and impediments to flow.
- The team members can make the list of metrics as flexible as they wish, considering other metrics that are relevant to a particular business process—metrics that help the team to see what is truly happening in the enterprise. Be creative!
- In many cases, the first value stream map the team creates will contain a great deal of estimated data because very little process performance data are collected in most offices. However, there is a message here: if the team sees the value in these metrics, it should consider establishing simple, quick ways of collecting some of the important ones on an ongoing basis to help manage the value stream within the context of a Lean enterprise.

Step 4: Perform Value Stream Walk-Through

This step is the main event for creating the current state map. It consumes most of the day, as the team uses this opportunity to understand how work is created, progresses, and is organized. The team members should make every effort to "walk" through this value stream from beginning to end, immersing themselves in the process. Ideally, the team observes each of the main process steps identified in Step 2 and collects the agreed-on data at each step. The team should feel free to ask questions necessary to identify issues and understand the work as it progresses and creates value.

The team will spend approximately 10 to 30 minutes for each process. Time spent will depend on the number of process boxes and the time allotted the walk-through. Some processes will take longer and others a shorter time based on what occurs at each. Having a team member act as time keeper here will keep the process moving along. Let's say the team determines that an average of 20 minutes per process is appropriate. The time keeper can keep the team aware of where they are at relative to that standard (e.g., "5 minutes to go"). The team members can decide if the current discussion is meaningful and should continue, or whether they are getting sidetracked or going too far into the details.

When the process time of a particular step is short relative to the time allotted each process then the team should observe the work being performed first-hand, perhaps conducting several observations as time allows. But what if the process time is long, say hours? It would be impossible to observe such processes during the mapping event. The team may choose to observe such processes in detail before or after the mapping event. During the event, the person who is performing the work can still describe what he or she does, how it is done, and the problems associated in the allotted time, though not actually performing the process. This is one of the tradeoffs that must be made on occasion.

Another tradeoff involves the *location* at which a process is performed. Perhaps a process is conducted offsite, even in another part of the world. How can a walk-through still be performed? It is possible to do "virtual walks," though they require additional preparations prior to the mapping event. The person performing the work should be part of the team. Ideally, he or she would travel to the site of the mapping event. Access to the various systems and information tools (forms, documents) must be prearranged. Then the person can demonstrate the work for the other team members. But what would still be missing is a sense of the work environment—the layout of the office, the interruptions or disruptions that may occur, and the like. Nonetheless, the person can describe these conditions. So although not ideal, a virtual tour may be a practical necessity.

Step 5: Establish How Each Process Prioritizes Work

During the walk-through, the mapping team should ask the people performing the work a simple question, "How do you prioritize your work?" "How do you know what to do next?" The responses are often interesting. The answers may also differ along the value stream. In other words, people may be working

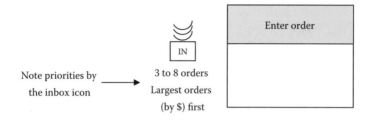

Figure 5.9 **Displaying priorities.**

toward different priorities. Remember that many resources in office and service processes perform multiple tasks. Therefore, the opportunity for conflicts in priorities increases. The response to the question of how people prioritize work is usually noted adjacent to the inbox icon, shown in Figure 5.9.

Step 6: Calculate System Summary Metrics

When the team has completed the walk-through (physical or virtual), it assesses the value stream performance from a systems perspective. The lead time and process times can be represented on a timeline at the bottom of the map, as shown in Figure 5.10. Each is summarized for the entire value stream. Although it's possible to document ranges of time in process data boxes, it's less confusing to average or take a midpoint of a range and note that on the timeline. Quality and cost metrics that the team has selected can also be summarized for the value stream. In Chapter 6 we will see how this is done for the Quick Loan Bank case study. The team should plan to use some of these metrics on a permanent basis to gauge the effectiveness and efficiency of the work within the future state designs. However, the team should take care not to create a massive data collection system to support the effort, instead keeping it simple and visual.

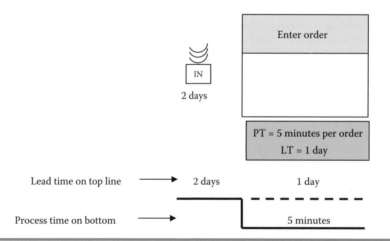

Figure 5.10 **Depicting process and lead time using a timeline.**

Step 7: Socialize the Map with Others Working in the Value Stream

Once the team completes the system metrics summary, the current state map represents the work as seen by this team. The gap here is that it represents only *the team's* view of the work and what its members saw and heard. There are others who have different experiences and views of reality than those who were assigned to map the value stream: their input is needed too, as it will give a more robust picture of the "real work" and barriers. It will also do one more important thing: by reaching out to get input from others, the rest of the affected organization will engage and begin to buy into the effort. We believe this "socialization" is critical to the success of any redesign we go through.

Once the team completes the initial visualization, consider this work a draft until others weigh in and give their perspectives. It's best to create a plan to socialize this with others in the organization who are involved in the value stream but not on the mapping team, and then approach them to get their input. So, consider reviewing the current state map with others at this point.

How do you engage the rest of the organization in changes? All successful change has technical and social components, and value stream mapping is a great example of a "social intervention." While the map provides a visual of the work, it also brings together different parts of the organization involved in flowing information and service to the customer. But relying on just a few people to grasp the situation and design a better value stream without organizational input is a recipe for failure: there are many realities in the organization, each valid in its own right.

A great way to incorporate other input is the process of socialization, which is defined as a cycle of communication, modification, and consensus building. In this process, each stakeholder has an opportunity to participate through deliberate discussions that surface thoughts, perspectives, and other people's realities. And, by seeking out these realities, we see immediate benefits in terms of

■ Confirming assumptions and data
■ Surfacing of hidden risks (technical or social)
■ Engaging the rest of the organization in problem solving.

We incorporate socialization with its own PDCA (*Plan–Do–Check–Act*) cycle as we continue to learn more about what is so hard to do: honing a process to communicate thoughts effectively and open dialogue about what is occurring, what might work, what we should try, etc.

Socialization is so critical to the success of redesigning a value stream that we use it at each step of the way, always engaging others and incorporating their thoughts. In this way it becomes embraced as "our" thinking, not "the mapping team's thinking."

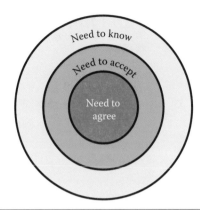

Figure 5.11 Levels of socialization.

When putting together a socialization plan, consider different levels of detail in the socialization, as depicted in Figure 5.11. Although people directly involved in the work *need to agree* on the team's work, those who are indirectly impacted may just *need to accept* that changes are underway. Finally, those who will not experience much impact at all may *need to know* what's going on as a general update in communicating the various changes being considered and implemented in your transformation.

The mapping tips in the following box sum up the discussion for Steps 3 through 7 in this chapter. The team can use these as a quick reference during mapping activities.

TIPS FOR MAPPING THE CURRENT STATE

- *Identify the basic process boxes before performing the actual walk-through.* This helps the team agree on the level of detail to use throughout the mapping. Included here is identifying the customers and suppliers (internal and/or external) to the identified value stream. This adequately sets boundaries for the mapping exercise by establishing the starting and ending points of the map. The team can add, subtract, or combine process boxes as necessary during the actual walk-through.

- *Identify the metrics that the team will collect for each process box.* At this point the team should agree on a definition for each metric. Doing this before the actual walk-through minimizes confusion and greatly speeds up the mapping process.

- *Add other information (via visual icons or metrics) as you observe the process steps in motion.* Be flexible, as there is no perfect current state map!

- *Guard against making the map too unwieldy; start simply and add boxes as necessary.* For example, if a series of activities is completed in a relatively short period (i.e., as compared to the overall expected lead time and the demand rate), use one process box to represent the entire group of activities.

- *Estimate the performance of the current state the first time through to get a quick picture of the value stream as it exists.* Most office and service processes have little true performance data, and it could take weeks or months to generate accurate data. Save the time and get estimates from the people who perform these tasks, or consider collecting these data in the weeks leading up to the mapping event.
- *Walk the value stream to gather the performance data associated with creating the value.* Mapping should *not* take place entirely in a meeting or conference room. Team members gain a higher level of knowledge as they personally witness each activity. Don't count on seeing all activities performed in minute detail: this is a high-level perspective. Observe the major tasks involved in the value stream, such as an actual order or an invoice being generated. Ask to see examples of the types of major problems that arise.
- *Ask questions regarding activities and issues you see to understand potential barriers in designing future states.* For example, there may be batching of paperwork at particular steps that may cause delays or create quality problems in subsequent steps. Why is work performed this way? Will this affect how the team thinks about the future state designs?
- *Map the whole value stream as a team.* If possible, avoid different people mapping different segments of the value stream. Understanding and seeing only a portion of the value stream creates a disconnected picture of the complete organization.
- *Assign team members specific tasks to perform in the mapping process.* This ensures that the mapping activities will be completed and the members stay engaged in the process. Ask one member to be the data recorder, making certain that the team fills out all metrics. Another member can be a scribe, recording any issues or ideas that are sure to arise during the walk-through. Still another member can be a timekeeper, measuring actual process times wherever possible and keeping the team on track.
- *Always draw by hand.* Drawing by hand creates minimal delay during the walk-through. In addition, it might be difficult to map and discuss the process performance at the same time. Therefore, always review the map to identify further information that you need and make changes before moving on. That's why we always use pencils and/or dry erase markers (and erasers)!
- *Remember the need to socialize before completing the map.* Value stream mapping is a social intervention, too! The experiences of others within the value stream are important not only to capture, but to also discuss. And, the increase in employee engagement will help make agreed-on changes easier to incorporate.

Chapter 6

Quick Loan Bank Current State

After some training and education in Lean and value stream mapping, the Quick Loan Bank mapping team reviewed the SIPOC (*S*uppliers–*I*nputs–*P*rocesses–*O*utputs–*C*ustomers) completed by the cross-functional management team prior to the mapping event (refer to Figure 4.2). The entire team understood that the focus was on used car loans and not on loans for new cars. Further, everyone understood the objectives of the event: to reduce turnaround time with no increase in employment. This in turn would result in a significant increase in loans, estimated to be 100%, or double the current number. All of this information was then used to socialize others within the identified service center and to seek their input and agreement. The team was now ready to draw the current state map.

Drawing the Current State Map

Step 1: Document Customer Information and Needs

The voice of the customer information reveals that customers need a same-day turnaround. An examination of Figure 4.1 reveals that customer demand can vary significantly from day to day; it is significantly higher on Saturdays and Mondays. Quick Loan Bank's current "win rate" is 8.5% as a percentage of loan applications. A total of 1400 applications per month are processed by the dealers by the specific loan center (remember, Quick Loan Bank has three) that is the subject of the value stream mapping exercise. The team learned from the dealers that they themselves reject 30% of the applications on the spot, using the same LoRisk software application that the underwriters use at Quick Loan Bank to do a preliminary credit check of the applicant. Therefore, 70% of, or 980, loan applications per month are electronically transferred to Quick Loan Bank.

The team captured this information on the current state map, as shown in Figure 6.1. The outside resource icon is used to represent the dealers. A data box below the icon contains the current demand, lead time expectations, and current "win rate" data.

Figure 6.1   **Customer icon and data box.**

Step 2: Identify the Main Process Boxes (in Order)

Dealers send loan applications through the LoRisk program Monday through Saturday between 8:00 A.M. and 6:00 P.M. The applications are received at the loan center. The applications are **reviewed** by underwriters to eliminate bad risks and "clean up" the applications. The underwriters reject 60% of the applications they review. All loan applications are passed on to the buyer, even the rejected ones.

The buyer **reviews** *all* applications as they are received from the underwriter. He or she notifies the dealer of any rejections via e-mail. For accepted applications, the buyer **sets the initial price and terms**. The buyer must obtain missing or incorrect information from the dealer on 50% of the accepted applications to do this. The buyer then **communicates** the loan terms back to the dealer electronically by way of the BankLoan program. The buyer may then **negotiate** the terms of the loan with the dealers (40% of loans are negotiated). The dealer and consumer **submit** the signed contract along with supporting documentation. Quick Loan Bank receives this signed contract for only 10.2% of the total number of loan applications. This documentation is **received** by a loan processor who **enters** the information into the BankLoan system, and who **verifies** the contract information. The loan processor must **contact** the dealer or consumer 80% of the time to obtain missing or incorrect documents. Once the required information is obtained, the loan processor will verify employment, salary, and insurance information by **contacting** the references provided. The loan processor can verify this information 75% of the time. Applications that cannot be verified are sent to a supervisor who will **process the exceptions**. After some investigation, the supervisor will reject 70% of those that he or she receives. Only 30% of the exceptions will be approved for funding.

The loan is then **funded** by the loan processor in the BankLoan system. On average, 83 loans per month are funded, which is equal to 8.5% of the total number of loan applications. Documentation is **scanned** into the BankLoan system and sent electronically to the bank's servicing group. The servicing group will contact the consumer to initiate loan payments. The physical documentation will be sent offsite for destruction. These last two processes are out-of-scope for this project, but the team thought it important to note them on the map nonetheless.

The main processes were identified as review loan application, review and set pricing and terms, communicate terms to dealer, negotiate loan, receive and verify contract from dealer/consumer, contact references such as employers and insurance companies, process exceptions, fund loan, and scan loan documentation. A process box will be drawn for each, for nine process boxes in total. This is shown in Figure 6.2.

Step 3: Select Process Metrics

Given the objective for the project—to reduce lead time while using the same resources to increase the win rate for used car auto loans and increase market share—the team selected the following business metrics:

■ Process time (PT), the time required to perform each process step, with no interruptions. Understanding the work content for each step will be important as the team wants to meet its turnaround time objective without increasing employment.

■ Lead time (LT), the time required to complete each process step, including any queue, wait, or delay time. The need to significantly reduce the turnaround time makes this metric very important. It will help the team to identify where there are delays in the value stream.

■ Complete and accurate (%C&A), the percentage of time that the information received from the previous step is complete and accurate. The team members understand that a frequent cause of delay is missing or incorrect information. Quantifying this will help them focus on where improvements are needed in this area.

■ The frequency as a percentage that various situations occur, such as approvals or rejections at particular points of the value stream.

■ The information technology used at each step.

■ The current monthly rate of demand or volume of applications and loans that are processed through each step, using an average over the previous three months.

■ The position involved at each step.

The team decided that it was unnecessary to note the number of people performing each step in the current state, as the expectation is that the volume will increase significantly in the future state. The team also decided that it was not worthwhile to note the number of current applications and loans in process throughout the value stream, as demand varies so significantly from day to day. This information would be of limited value, and therefore would not be included on the map. The team is confident that the metrics selected will give them the information they need to understand the current state value stream and to identify the key issues of flow and waste.

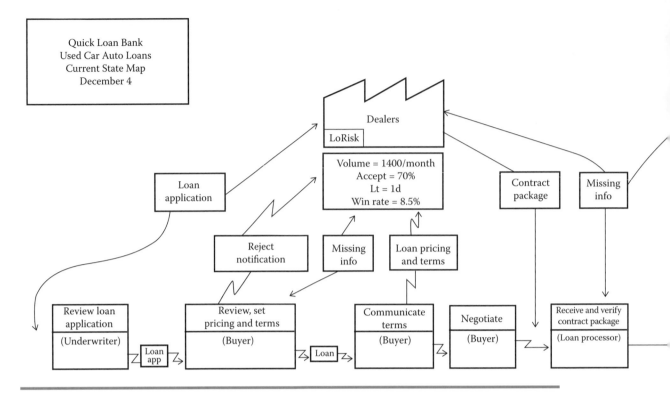

Figure 6.2   (A) Current state map with main process boxes in order.   *(Continued)*

Step 4: Perform Value Stream Walk-Through, Fill In Data Boxes

The team performed a walk-through of the value stream. Each process step was observed as it was actually being performed so that the entire team gained a common and accurate understanding. The observations were made at someone's desk, cubicle, or office whenever possible. At times the observation took place in the conference room where the team was meeting. When this was necessary, team members still had to demonstrate the work and the systems and tools that they were using. At times it was not practical to observe the work. For example, the "negotiating loan" step was discussed in a conference room. Team members were relied on to describe this step, drawing on their experience. Everyone was encouraged to ask questions of each other during the observations and discussions. Very importantly, they asked for specific examples of the type of information that was missing or was incorrect.

A data box for each process step was filled in, including any data collected prior to the event. The team members understood from the training they had received that there was more than one correct way to display the data, and quickly agreed on ways to depict particular data consistently on the map. The data collected are summarized in Table 6.1. Note that process time (PT) is expressed in minutes (m) and lead time (LT) is expressed in days (d). Figure 6.3 shows the current state map, with the data boxes added.

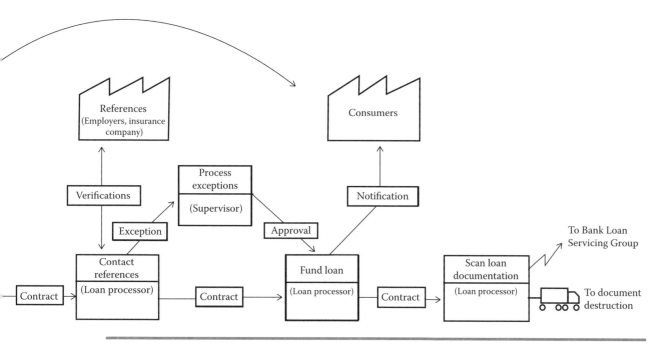

Figure 6.2 (Continued) **(B) Current state map with main process boxes in order.**

Step 5: Establish How Each Process Prioritizes Work

The team asked this important question at each step of the process and received a consistent response throughout. Everyone said that they simply completed the work on whatever application or loan arrived first into the queue. In other words, everyone processed work on a "first-in-first-out," or FIFO basis. The team felt that this was a positive practice in general and depicted it on the current state map with a note at each queue or inbox icon prior to each process step (see Figure 6.4).

Step 6: Calculate the System Metrics for the Value Stream

The team totaled the process and lead times for each step. Two expressions of lead time were calculated. First, the team calculated the lead time from receipt of the loan application to notification that the loan had been funded—the most important detail for the dealer and consumer. In addition, they calculated the lead time for the Servicing group by simply adding the time to scan the loan documentation, as the bank has an interest in this overall lead time. The average total process time and average total lead times for the value stream were recorded on the current state map (refer to Figure 6.4). In addition, the team calculated an overall %C&A for the entire value stream by

Table 6.1 **Current State Process Data**

Process Step	PT (min)	LT (days)	C&A (%)	Info Tech	Monthly Volume	Position
Review loan application	15	0.1–0.25	100	LoRisk	980	Underwriter
Review, set pricing, and terms	4–14	0.1–0.2	50	BankLoan	980	Buyer
Communicate terms to dealer	4–6	0–0.2	100	BankLoan	392	Buyer/underwriter
Negotiate loan	6–10	0	100	Phone	157	Buyer/dealer
Receive and verify contract package	25	0.1–0.5	20	E-mail	100	Loan processor
Contact references	10	1–4	75	Phone/BankLoan	100	Loan processor
Process exceptions	0–10	0–0.25	100	BankLoan	25	Supervisor
Fund loan	1	0.1–0.2	100	BankLoan	83	Loan processor
Scan loan documentation	5	3–4	100	BankLoan	83	Loan processor

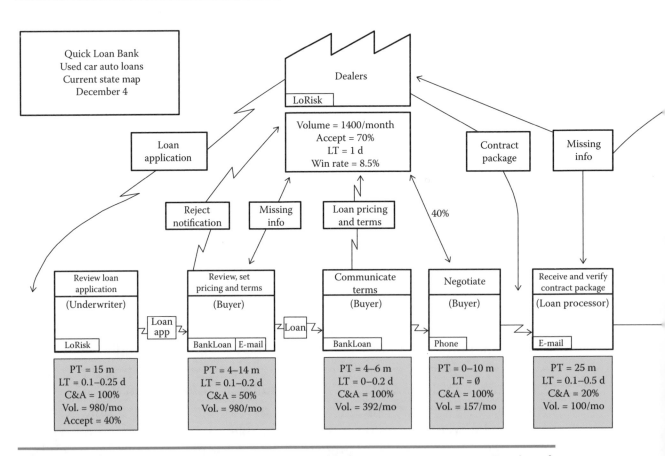

Figure 6.3 (A) Current state map with data boxes added. **(Continued)**

multiplying together the decimal equivalent of the %C&A for each process step as follows:

$$\text{Overall \%C\&A} = 1.0 \times 0.5 \times 1.0 \times 1.0 \times 0.2 \times 0.75 \times 1.0 \times 1.0 \times 1.0 = \underline{7.5\%}$$

The team's initial reaction to this figure was one of surprise. Only 7% to 8% of all of the loan applications and loans go through the value stream *without* some form of missing or incorrect information. The percentage measures the defect and correction waste in the value stream. Missing and incorrect information significantly impedes the flow of applications and loans and creates a great deal of non-value-added work for everyone. This clearly must be addressed in the future state.

Step 7: Socialize the Current State Map

The completed current state map is shown in Figure 6.4. Of course it should still be considered a draft until it has been shared with others working in the value stream and everyone is satisfied that it truly depicts what is currently happening. The team decided to share the current state map at this point and receive any additional input that may be important before moving on to develop the future state. But first, they reflected as a team on the current state map. What had they

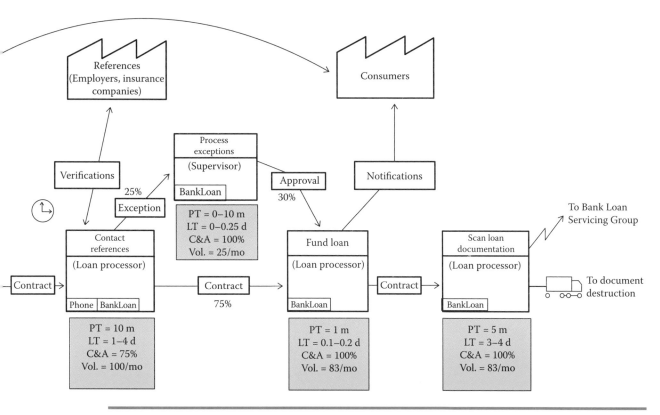

Figure 6.3 (Continued) **(B) Current state map with data boxes added.**

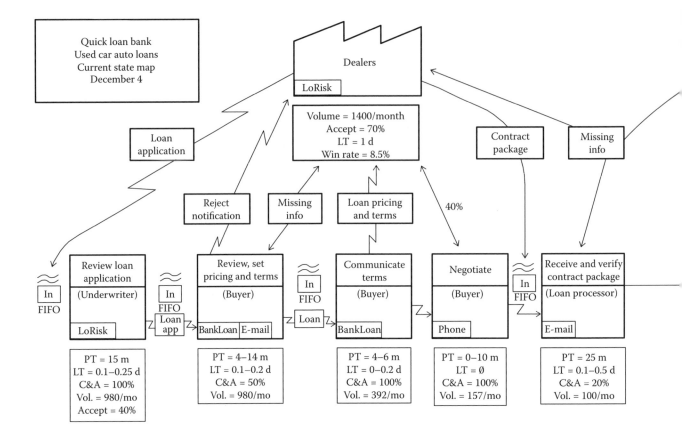

Figure 6.4   (A) Completed current state map.   *(Continued)*

learned from everything they observed and heard? What do the data tell them? What key issues of flow are there? What are the key wastes that are keeping them from meeting their goals? Each team member had a chance to contribute to the discussion. Here is a partial list.

- Much lead time from receiving the application to notifying the consumer (circa 3.5 days on average), very little work content (circa 1.5 hours)
- Very low %C&A for the value stream (circa 7% to 8%) that is requiring extra work for everyone to correct
- Several different groups involved in answering a simple question: Should we approve this application?

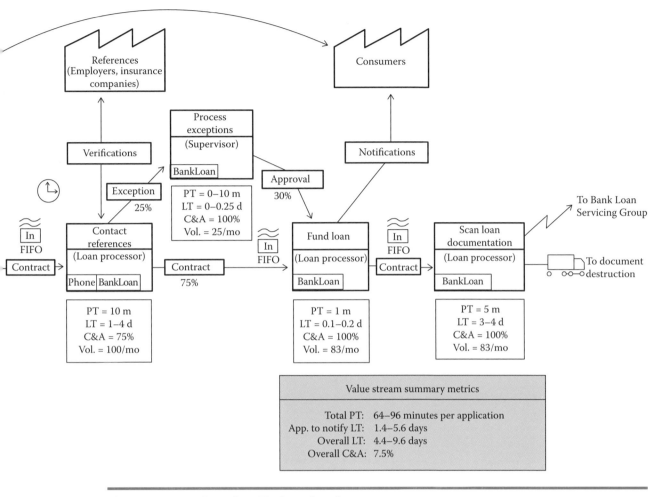

Figure 6.4 (Continued)   (B) Completed current state map.

- High failure rate for loan deals with little analysis of why so many loan applications fail to become loans
- Inconsistency in decisions to reject applications and in setting loan terms
- Volumes are significantly higher on Saturdays and Mondays (circa 53% received on just two days of the week)

The team members shared these reflections, along with the current state map, when they met with others in the organization, asking for other perspectives from the groups to get a sense of their current state realities. Next, they made any necessary changes based on the input they received, turning it from a draft into a completed current state map. Now it's on to the future state!

Chapter 7

Designing a Future State

We covered the benefits of current state mapping in Chapter 5: development of a common understanding of how the process currently functions, identification of wastes and issues of flow, and even improved cross-functional relations. These are all good things. However, the real power of value stream mapping is in the development of the future state map, or a common vision of how the service line should operate. The future state map is the opportunity for the team to redefine the process to meet specific business objectives defined by management during the preparation activity prior to the mapping event. The mapping team may expose many opportunities during the current state mapping effort, but an organization typically doesn't have all the resources necessary to address all opportunities at once. So, the question becomes: How and where do we start?

MAPPING TIP

When designing a future state, the mapping team will always identify several alternatives—there is no single correct future state. However, the team can narrow its selection by designing a future state that directly applies to the business goals of the enterprise and that the company can implement in a reasonable time frame (typically three to six months).

To begin designing the organization's future state, the team should revisit the initial business objectives and review the current state map, along with the reflections resulting from it. We then suggest that the team consider the set of future state questions in Box 7.1 as a guideline to developing a future state. Collectively, the questions represent a thought process that will guide the team in identifying the opportunities to apply Lean concepts to any value stream in the organization. We'll examine each of these questions in the following sections and then apply them to the Quick Loan Bank case study in Chapter 8.

When engaging the future state questions, it is not always necessary to follow the exact sequence shown, but there is a reason that they are presented in this order. For example, Question 2 prompts the team to identify the key wastes that

---

BOX 7.1 FUTURE STATE QUESTIONS

1. What does the customer really need?
2. Which steps create value and which generate waste?
3. How can work flow with fewer interruptions?
4. How will interruptions in the flow be controlled?
5. How will the workload and/or activities be leveled?
6. How will we manage the new process?
7. What process improvements will be necessary to achieve the future state?

---

need to be eliminated, or at least reduced. It only makes sense to discuss waste before moving on to Question 3, which involves improving flow, because of course we do not want to flow waste more effectively. Similarly, we want to improve flow and reduce the number or magnitude of interruptions (Question 3) before we consider how to control work when interruptions occur (Question 4). When customer needs in the form of the demand on the process vary, the discussion is likely to move quickly into ways to level that demand if possible (Question 5).

The key is that practitioners need to make sure that they have addressed each question during the design of the future state. The questions represent the key Lean concepts: waste, flow, pull, leveling, and management timeframe or pitch. Only if they are all considered will the team be assured that it is significantly changing the way that work flows and is managed.

MAPPING TIP

It has been our experience that many value stream mapping efforts fail to use the future state questions to guide the redesign process. Instead, teams and organizations choose to identify the myriad wastes that exist in the current state: dozens of improvement opportunities are noted on the current state map; a list of these opportunities is created and prioritized; and people are then assigned responsibility to follow up on each. This approach is best described as a "waste war." Although providing some benefit to the organization, it often fails to change the fundamental flow of the process and the way it is managed and does not provide the sustainable breakthrough results we have come to expect when redesigning value streams based on Lean thinking. Practitioners are strongly encouraged to use the approach described in this chapter.

Question 1: What Does the Customer Really Need?

Since Lean is market driven, it's not surprising that we begin by asking this question. The following subquestions dig more deeply into customer needs and will provoke a more thoughtful response from the team:

- Who needs the output of the process?
- What is specifically required? How often is it required?
- When do they need the output?

In other words, what specifically do customers need and when do they need it? Remember, we are designing a *future* state. Let's say that the demand on the value stream is expected to change substantially in the future. The value stream mapping team must consider this while designing the future state. It would be unwise to design a future state for historic demand if demand is expected to increase or decrease significantly in the future. Let's say that demand on a loan process is expected to increase by 100% over the next year or so. The value stream mapping team needs to design the future state with this in mind. It will prompt the team to focus its redesign efforts accordingly. For example, the team may focus its discussion of waste (Question 2) at key steps where there will likely be a struggle to keep up at the higher volume. Appendix II provides interested readers a more in-depth review of the subject of demand and demand rates.

So which customers are we referring to? Customers here can be "external" or "internal." External customers are the end users who purchase the outputs and services that are created by the value stream. Internal customers are the various departments and functions within the value stream that perform the activities required. Understanding and meeting the needs of *internal* customers so that the needs of the *external* customers can be met is critically important. This requires a collaborative approach by the value stream team, among members representing the various functions and departments. Key opportunities for improvement in the current state often exist at the major interfaces between internal customers in the value stream. There will certainly be some give and take between the internal customers regarding the lead time that each requires to complete his or her segment of the value stream, as well as which activities should be done at particular points of the value stream. This give and take must always be conducted in the context of the needs of the external customers, which are usually not negotiable.

Clearly defining information and service requirements for *each major segment* of the value stream is important to ensure flow with fewer interruptions. This is particularly important at the major interfaces between internal customers. A good practice to follow at this point is to first identify the major segments, or "chunks," of the value stream.

Breaking Down Future State Thinking: Chunking the Map with Purpose

At this point, the current state map has visualized work and pointed to many problems. Teams are often overwhelmed and don't know where to begin to redesign the work. What the current state indicates are real problems in being

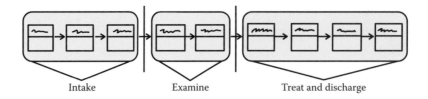

Figure 7.1   **Identifying major segments or chunks of a value stream.**

■ Effective (giving the customer what is needed) with the output
■ Efficient (not running into each other or spinning your wheels) in creating the output

It can help a team to make sense out of the current state chaos by standing back and taking a broader view of the map to see the major elements of the value stream. For example, as you might imagine, there is a great deal of activity in an Emergency Department (ED) of a hospital, but from a higher altitude it's possible to describe the work in a few major steps:

■ We intake patients into our facility.
■ We examine their condition.
■ We treat and discharge them.

These segments would be noted on the map as shown in Figure 7.1.

When looking at the ED from this perspective, we are identifying critical internal handoffs that can make or break its ability to be both effective and efficient. The benefit of this type of thinking is that we can clearly identify points in the future state where we can design key internal customer requirements to improve the flow of work. We call this analysis "chunking," as each of the high-level steps (in this example: intake, examine, and treat and discharge) are major segments, or "chunks," of the value stream, each with its own distinctive needs.

As we design the future state, we spend significant time understanding both the end customer's needs and the internal customer requirements of each chunk. This aligns our thinking as a focus on the rest of the future state redesign!

MAPPING TIP

Separate chunks usually revolve around such characteristics as

■ Handoffs to different functions (admission to hospital bed, sales to order processing)
■ Handoffs to different offices (field office transactions sent to central accounting, partial designs sent to another design center)
■ Handoffs to different capabilities (basic tax preparation forwarded to a CPA, vendor solicitation progressing to negotiating)

■ Major changes in the work content (prospecting potential sales opportunities turning into quotes, testing product designs progressing to finalizing the designs)

Establishing Customer Requirements Using Chunks

This step of future state mapping is usually the most eye opening for mapping teams in that they discuss, often for the first time, what the REAL requirements are inside and at the end of the value stream. What we've found is that the real surprises are imbedded in the internal requirements: many of the teams have legacy processes, where everyone assumed that they were meeting the requirements of the person to whom they were sending the work. Chances are, you believe that right now for the work you do. But what response do you think you would get if you asked the recipient of your work how often it arrived with the right timing, content, and accuracy for him or her to proceed without a pause? The response to this question is captured in the Percent Complete and Accurate (%C&A) metric on the current state map for each process box. Breaking down these assumptions and having rich conversations about today's process requirements, as well as future process requirements, is both critical and enlightening. So how do we go about doing this?

Step 1: Identify, Draw, and Label the Chunks

The best way we've found is to have the team identify the chunks from the current state map. Value stream maps that involve many departments typically have three or four chunks. Less complicated ones may have only two. Once the chunks are decided on, the team will identify them on the future state map, noting the name for each chunk in terms of the work (in the form of a verb) that occurs in that chunk. For instance, the ED example in Figure 7.1 would have three chunks: *intake, examine, and treat and discharge.*

MAPPING TIPS

When determining chunks, identify the boundaries within which the team is comfortable. However, the team members might decide to redefine the boundaries as they think through new designs. Each chunk typically has several process boxes grouped into one chunk of related work. Consider keeping the number of chunks to just a few, typically two to four, depending on how broad the scope of work is. Draw vertical lines on the map where the boundaries of the chunks are and name them with active verbs describing the work (as opposed to the outcome of the work).

Refrain from making too many assumptions about the chunks. For instance,

- Just because we have a chunk in the current state doesn't mean we want to keep it in the future state: it may provide little value as we rethink the flow of work.
- The order of the chunks may change to benefit either internal or external requirements for effectiveness and efficiency.

Step 2: Define and Document Requirements at Each Chunk Interface

Now that we have identified chunks, it's time to create a list of internal and external requirements for the value stream, as depicted in Figure 7.2. The best way we've found to do this is to

- Clearly identify the needs of the external customer in terms of timing, content, and so on, as information exits the value stream
- Clearly identify the needs of the first chunk as information enters the value stream
- Recognize the drawn lines of the chunks as major interfaces (and handoffs) of work
- Arrange the supplier and customer of the interfaces to work together in understanding the customer requirements of each chunk interface
- Clearly identify the needs of the "receiving chunk" of work/information from the "supplying chunk" within the value stream
- If possible, write the requirements down on or below the map at the point of the interface

This discussion usually takes a while (give yourself at least 90 minutes), as this is the first time many people have had this discussion and the social aspects of talking this through are critical. Typical requirements about the work/information might include

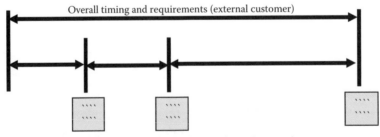

Overall timing and requirements (external customer)

Clearly define the timing and requirements for each internal customer

Figure 7.2 **Noting lead time, Complete and Accurate data, and other requirements at major interfaces.**

- Quantity
- Cost
- Timing
- Format of information
- Source of information (e.g., what file or data base is required)

Many teams have found it helpful to mock up formats/forms/screens to clearly define needs. Do whatever seems to be good for the discussion!

Step 3: Decide on How Many Chunks You Want/Need to Redesign

At this point, you've had a great discussion about fundamental information and work requirements within and without the value stream. Now it's time to focus your direction! Instead of assuming that all chunks need redesign and attention, why not determine how many you *should* work on? This is a straightforward exercise, but not necessarily a straightforward discussion, as consensus is needed by the cross-functional team to proceed!

A great way to begin this discussion is to revisit the scoping document and the objectives defined for the value stream redesign effort. Consider those objectives now in the context of how the team sees the chunks and chunk requirements. The team's reconciliation discussion now revolves around:

- How big a gap do we have in our current state versus the required performance in the (near-term) future?
- What are the alternatives in addressing the chunk requirements in terms of:
  - Meeting the required value stream performance?
  - Capacities and limitations in meeting chunk requirements?
  - Social acceptance of meeting chunk requirements?
- How many/which chunks might be the best selection to meet the overall performance requirements?

Once the team has agreed on the answers to these questions, the remaining future state design questions can be applied to just those selected chunks: there is no need to draw a better work flow on a map for a chunk that is not being included in this first wave of future state work! This will limit future state mapping overproduction and keep the team focused on good designs in the areas of interest.

LEAN EXAMPLE

A value stream mapping event was conducted for a hiring process at an organization. At the outset of the development of the future state the external customer, a hiring manager, was asked, "What specific lead time do you need when hiring for an existing position?" The response was, "Since people provide a two-week notice before they depart, I would like a qualified candidate hired, oriented, and provided some basic instruction in two weeks." The value stream mapping team then worked backward from this goal to determine specific lead time goals for the pre-hire, the interview and selection, and the post-hire segments of the value stream. This, in turn, generated creative ideas of how these intermittent goals could be met and, in turn, the seemingly impossible goal of two weeks for the overall value stream (in this case, hiring, orienting, and providing some basic instruction to a new candidate). The team began to identify the *minimal* needs to perform specific activities sooner in the value stream with little or no risk and in parallel with other activities. This helped them to collapse the overall lead time to the goal defined by the external customer. Much give and take took place, but at no time did the team lose sight of the overall objective defined by the customer.

Question 2: Which Steps Create Value and Which Generate Waste?

There is some amount of waste in every process. The key here is to focus attention during discussion of this question to the key points in the value stream, and keep the discussion at the appropriate scale. As previously stated, the team wants to avoid going on a "waste war"—addressing *all* waste in the current state. For a month-end closing example, let's say that a goal is to perform the process with eight full-time equivalents, rather than ten. Let's also say that the total process time is 240 hours. So, the team must identify opportunities to reduce the process time from 240 hours per close to 196 hours, a difference of 48 hours. The team should not be concerned with opportunities of several minutes when the objective is to reduce process time by 48 hours. And certainly the team will want to focus its attention at the identified bottlenecks or constraints. Focus is critical here.

To root out these wastes, the team should challenge the work within a value stream by asking the following:

- Why are the current steps being performed?
- What can the company do differently (or not at all) while still meeting customer needs?
- Is the order of steps creating waste? At what steps should decisions be made?
- What assumptions underlie the design of the current process?
- Are current controls and administrative guidelines appropriate?
- What knowledge and skills are truly required to perform the steps?

It might be important to unravel the history of the existing system to identify the particular rules and assumptions that underlie the current structure. For example, the organization may have set up a system to accommodate the skill level of particular individuals whom it no longer employs. Or maybe there is an assumption that the management information system can work only a certain way, so the company designed the process around this limitation, but meanwhile, a subsequent version of the software had corrected the problem. In some cases, current practices are a result of administrative controls, such as excessive approvals, the company established in the past. Is there still a need for them? What are their costs versus their perceived benefits?

Another area of non-value-adding activity is relying on a high skill level to perform a task when lesser skills might be satisfactory (or vice versa!). There may be a way to simplify and standardize an activity so other, or fewer, people can perform it. Information system–based solutions and technologies, as well as documented standardized work, may eliminate reliance on employees' knowledge of specialized information—what's called "tribal knowledge"—to execute the current system. The organization might be able to eliminate entire processes, or at least automate them, by the application of such solutions.

Correction waste is often the focus of the first future state. The Complete and Accurate (C&A) data on the current state map, and the overall C&A for the value stream will indicate the magnitude of this waste. Ideas to address correction waste are identified here, during discussion of Question 2. Checklists, mistake-proofing methods, and other techniques are often identified for the future state. Without a high level of information and service quality, the value stream will never adequately flow.

The value stream mapping team must challenge "legacy" non-value-adding practices so that they don't become part of the future state. In our experience, this often isn't done. A good question to ask here is, "Are there any activities that we really just shouldn't do?" It is always better, whenever possible, to eliminate an activity altogether than to reduce the time spent on it. By eliminating unnecessary activities, the opportunity for a queue to form is eliminated, and this in turn improves flow, which leads us to the third future state question.

Question 3: How Can Work Flow with Fewer Interruptions?

Most organizations are under pressure from customers and markets to deliver services in less time. In the absence of such pressure, there can still be reasons that an organization wants to improve flow. This fact makes the Lean concept of "flow" very important. Commonly, a review of the current state reveals piles of work being sent downstream and "tossed over the wall" to the next process, which creates long lead times for the office and service value streams. The current state often includes numerous interruptions, as indicated by the multiple queue icons throughout the value stream. Further, these interruptions occur for a myriad of reasons.

As we discussed in Question 2, poor information and service quality is a common cause of disruptions in flow. People have to return to a prior step or the "supplier" of the information or service to obtain the correct or missing information. Remember, from the discussion of Question 1, the team may have identified that a bottleneck or constraint exists within the value stream. Queues of work typically accumulate prior to a constraint. The team will have discussed ideas to reduce process time and relieve the bottleneck in Question 2. Here, in Question 3, we explore other reasons for interruptions.

One reason can be "batch processing," which relates to the frequency that a process is performed. An organization may have valid reasons for batch processing, such as people supporting several value streams or multitasking. Figure 7.3 compares and contrasts large or infrequent batch processing versus smaller or more frequent batch processing.

Referring to Figure 7.3, let's say that A, B, and C are different types of office or service processes (e.g., invoices, receipts, and a general ledger). Also let's assume that the same person is responsible for performing each (i.e., multitasking). On the left side of the figure, each process is performed once a week. This may be the case because it works best for the person performing these tasks, or it might just be because "we've always done it that way." This practice means that two of the processes wait while the person performs the third one. How long they wait will depend on the frequency with which each process is performed. In this example, the waiting and therefore the lead time can be up to one week.

The right side of the figure shows each process being performed each day, or in smaller batches at a time, resulting in reduced lead time and other desirable outcomes, such as improved flexibility. Certainly, creating an invoice every day is more timely and efficient than creating several once a week. Therefore, the question remains as to the appropriate frequency. Weekly? Daily? Hourly? The answer

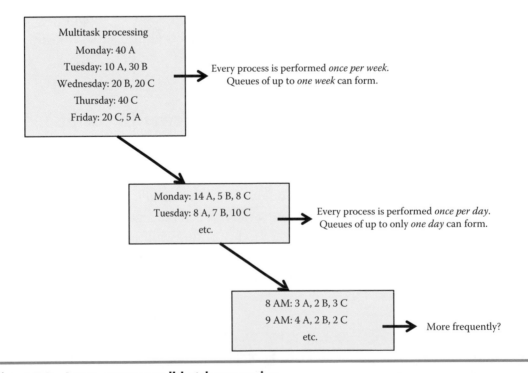

Figure 7.3 Large- versus small-batch processing.

to this question will depend on the desired service levels and goals identified in Question 1. For example, if the goal is to process invoices within a day, we cannot perform the invoicing process weekly. The team must identify and resolve any existing barriers to smaller batch processing so that the desired goals can be met.

Another potential cause of interruption is the number of handoffs in the current state. For each handoff there is a potential for a queue to form, as seen in Figure 7.4 on the left-hand side. In some cases it may be desirable to combine steps and have them performed by a single person to eliminate handoffs, as shown on the right-hand side.

Several factors must be taken into account when considering this approach to improving flow. The complexity of the work is one consideration. Will combining the processes create overly complex work that isn't reasonable for a single person to perform? We suggest not being too quick to discard this possibility, as the benefits can be significant in terms of improved flow and customer service. Think about "help desk"-type services. No customer is pleased when he or she is transferred to another person when the first service provider is unable to solve the problem. In this case, perhaps troubleshooting guides or other tools could be created to allow for more problems to be solved by the first service provider.

If combining processes is possible, a discussion of the capacity needed to meet expected demand should take place to determine the number of people required. To recall, we covered this briefly in Question 1 (and cover it in more depth in Appendix II). If it is not possible, there are other alternatives to flow.

Figure 7.5 displays a cross-functional co-located team approach on the right-hand side: a single team, single process concept. Team members are located together, and, very important, the work has been balanced between them. Only with adequate balancing will the potential for queues be minimized.

We assume here that team members are dedicated to the processes involved whenever they are being performed. Note the term "whenever." The approach can even be applied to value streams that are performed periodically, such as the

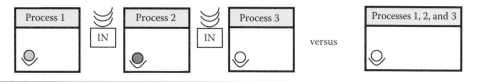

Figure 7.4 **Batch and queue processing versus combining activities.**

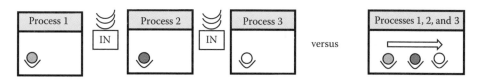

Figure 7.5 **Batch and queue processing versus cross-functional, co-located teams.**

month-end-closing process used as an example earlier in this chapter. In other words, it's applicable not only to high transactional, high-frequency processes.

Many industries have realized the significant benefits of uninterrupted flow by establishing multifunctional office or service teams organized in production-like cells in such processes as order processing (e.g., from order to invoice), product design (e.g., concurrent engineering), bidding and proposal teams, and contract administration. Many organizations have seen tangible benefits, such as reduced lead time, improved information and service quality, and greater flexibility. These quality benefits are typically a result of improved communication between team members because of the co-locating nature of the approach.

Yet another approach to flow is concurrency. Perhaps it is possible to perform processes or entire segments of the value stream in parallel to others. This is depicted in Figure 7.6. Parallel processing is a flow concept because it can result in a decrease in lead time. As discussed in Question 1, it is important to define specifically the information and service needs for each major segment of the value stream. We often discover the possibility for parallel processing during that discussion. A good question to ask is "what do we minimally need to start a process or segment with no or little risk of creating other problems downstream at a later time?"

Controlling the amount of work-in-process (WIP) throughout the value stream is another key concept of flow. It has been our experience that, too often, people are working on too many things at the same time (relatively speaking). Excessive WIP can significantly increase lead time. The more work in the "pipeline" or value stream, the longer it will take for any form of work to make its way through. Further, the possibility for interruptions *increases* with more WIP. For example, the likelihood that a change in priorities will occur will increase with more WIP. Therefore, we recommend minimizing the amount of WIP to reduce the possibility for disruptions and allow people to focus on the work that is in front of them. When there is less WIP at any time, there is less danger of switching between orders, projects, or any form of work, really.

Our ideal scenario is to eliminate all interruptions in flow, but this is not always possible. At this point, the discussion should move to identifying points in the value stream where interruptions can still occur, and how to control them. We cover this in Question 4.

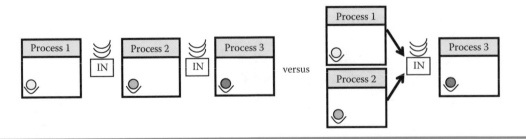

Figure 7.6 **Performing activities concurrently or in parallel.**

Question 4: How Will Interruptions in the Flow Be Controlled?

Office and service work typically progresses through a value stream, with each step "throwing it over the wall" to the next step. In many cases, the person receiving this work might not be available or might be overwhelmed with other work, resulting in the work being interrupted and queued in an inbox. We call this type of progression a "push system."

The flow concepts covered in Question 3 can relieve this issue, as the organization finds ways to combine tasks and/or people to allow work to progress without queues. However, there are times when flow is not possible: the person receiving the work might be responsible for tasks outside the value stream, or might be located some distance away. It makes sense to find a way to smooth the impact of interrupted flow to improve the system performance. By establishing simple and visual rules, organizations can prevent one part of the value stream from getting too far ahead of another. That is, instead of pushing work forward, it's possible to *pull* it forward, allowing work to progress only when the next step is ready for it.

One method that utilizes the concept of pull is a "sequential pull lane." This is the type of pull system most commonly used in office and service environments. When there is an interruption and a queue forms, it's possible that service providers within the value stream can select what to work on next. We need to define the desired sequence of work so that everyone is working to the correct priorities. Most often, the desired sequence is "first-in-first-out" (FIFO). However, in a project environment the desired sequence might be by due date. There's no reason to be working on a project due a year from now when there is a project of similar complexity due in the next six months. In an emergency room at a hospital, the desired sequence is severity of condition, identified as part of a triage step. The key is to define the desired sequence and represent it visually, to be certain that everyone is working to consistent priorities.

Sequential pull lanes not only prioritize what work to do next, but also establish a maximum amount of work that can be queued between tasks. For instance, if there was an FIFO lane allowing two projects to queue between two process steps, Step 1 could not work on any more projects if there were already two projects in the FIFO lane (see Figure 7.7). That person would either find something else to do or help the person at Step 2 to move the work along the

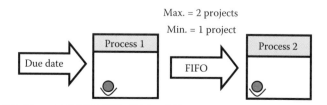

Figure 7.7 Sequential pull system.

value stream. This is considered a pull because Step 1 can't move work forward unless Step 2 is ready for it, eliminating overproduction from Step 1. Of course, there is a small queue of work that can ebb and flow to a maximum of two and a minimum of one. Despite the effort to balance capacity to demand throughout the value stream (Questions 1 and 3), there can still be situations in which an interruption in flow can arise because demand exceeds capacity at a particular point in time. The response triggered by a pull system can keep the interruption to an acceptable level.

This leads to another benefit of pull—control of the amount of WIP through the value stream. There is a relationship between lead time and the amount of WIP. The more work that is in-process and in queues throughout the value stream, the *longer* it will take to make its way through the value stream. Often the amount of WIP in the current state will vary significantly, as no rules or limits have been established. By controlling the size of the queues, the result is a more stable and predictable value stream from a lead time perspective. This can provide important benefits to the organization, along with improved customer service.

To determine the appropriate amount of WIP at a step, the team must consider the timing they defined for each step (or entire chunks) back in Question 1. It is often not a matter of "how many?" but rather "how long?" How long can work sit and wait to be handled before established timing goals will not be met? If a step or steps in the value stream aren't completed within the desired timing, then the service goal to the external customer will in all likelihood not be met. Therefore, at this point, it is very helpful to revisit the decisions made in Question 1. By drawing on this information, we can establish the maximum allowable queues at key points in the value stream; if reached, this will trigger a reallocation of resources or some other decision to be made to ensure that overall service goals are maintained.

By using pull systems with visual signals that trigger work, the organization can support teams in meeting their objectives and assisting with the reallocation of resources to make sure that people are working on the right thing at the right time. Organizations in various industries have successfully applied pull concepts to office and service processes including, but not limited to, order processing, product design, accounting, purchasing, distribution operations, healthcare, and retail operations.

LEAN EXAMPLE

Another example of pull is to print information only on demand, allowing modifications and updates to occur without affecting the downstream process. For example, modifications to engineering drawings have less impact on purchasing if they are printed out only when purchasing is ready to act on the drawing. Customer orders can also change frequently in many businesses: management can apply simple and visual pull concepts to minimize the impact of these changes, printing the information only when it's time to process the order. Both of these examples meet the objective of pull, which is to produce work only when needed by the next process or customer.

Question 5: How Will the Workload and/or Activities Be Leveled?

Work typically requires leveling from two perspectives: the process and the system. At the process level, there are people who overproduce in big batches, creating queues at the next step. At the system level, there are lopsided transactions and activities (such as month-end activities) that require different amounts of system resources at different points in time. Both types of imbalance create serious problems for the value stream as people must make significant adjustments to the daily efforts, and lead times can get very long.

Work at a process level can be balanced inside a value stream by using techniques such as flow and pull, which we covered in Questions 3 and 4. All of these focus on absorbing and reacting to changes in the work to enable a smooth progression through the value stream. Techniques are also available to level the workload on the overall system. For example, it may be possible for an organization to influence customer demand patterns. At a company that manufactures windows for homes, "cut-off days" for orders were given to each customer in a way that resulted in a more consistent number of orders taken each day. This helped level the demand on office personnel processing orders. Incentives have often been used to affect customer-buying patterns for the purpose of leveling demand. "Early bird specials" used by restaurants is one such example. Leveling is a key Lean concept. It seeks to distribute the same work over a longer period. Establishing a more consistent workload, where possible, creates a very predictable enterprise and improves the visibility and responsiveness to problems and/or minor shifts in customer demand.

Determining the correct mix of transactions can also improve the ability of the system to flow or respond to particular steps—for example, determining the ideal number of rush orders versus standard orders to process. In addition, adjusting the volume of transactions (demand variation) can root out inefficiencies in the system. Let's consider the month-end-close process, which we've referred to periodically in this chapter. Our experience has shown that we don't have to wait until the end of the month to perform up to 50% of the work required in the process. The work can be leveled throughout the month, thus reducing the significant increase of workload on accounting and other resources at the beginning of each month.

It is not always possible to level the workload, however. There can still be high telephone call volumes at particular times of the day. Demand on urban hospital emergency rooms will be higher on weekends. The demand on insurance companies will surely spike during natural disasters. Such organizations have learned to reduce, not eliminate, the impact of unleveled demand on the system. For example, many hospitals now track and publish current wait times in their emergency rooms. Ambulance services have learned to check these wait times before selecting the hospital to which to take a patient in need of emergency care. This levels the demand on the entire healthcare system within a region. Although there are usually no simple solutions, the team has an opportunity here to realize significant benefits for the company if creative approaches can be identified.

Question 6: How Will We Manage the New Process?

By now, the team has designed a future state that has significantly changed the flow of work and how it is to be performed. At this point, the discussion moves to how the new value stream will be managed. This subject is often overlooked and is a common cause of the inability to sustain the changes envisioned in the future state. There's a fundamental reason for this: if the company designs a system to perform to customer requirements, it will need to check frequently for abnormalities that hinder this performance and then create corrective actions (countermeasures) to get the work back on track.

So, what is a reasonable management timeframe or "pitch" for the value stream? In other words, how frequently will we check the performance or the "pulse" of the value stream? In an office and service environment, it can be somewhat arbitrary. Let's go back to the month-end-closing example. Let's say that the goal is to close in three days. How long does the organization want to wait before it determines whether the process is performing to expectations and will meet the three-day goal? Management would certainly not wait until the end of the closing cycle to discover that there is a problem—valuable time would be lost forever. In this case, management might select four hours as a reasonable timeframe for checking the performance of the process (Lean enterprises tend to have very short management timeframes).

As the team thinks through new Lean behaviors, it shouldn't spend a great deal of time checking the performance of the system. Instead, it should determine simple ways to provide performance visibility at key points in the value stream. Team members themselves can serve as the visual signal of abnormalities in the value stream. In a Lean culture, everyone is encouraged to bring abnormalities or nonstandard conditions to the attention of leaders in a timely manner. This requires a "safe" environment in which all associates feel comfortable speaking up. How safe they feel will depend on the response from leaders, which brings us to another key point. Visibility in itself is insufficient. When undesirable conditions arise, they must trigger a supportive response.

LEAN EXAMPLE

A printing company developed a goal of a three-day turnaround on orders, with a one-day turnaround in the preproduction portion of the order. They decided on a two-hour management timeframe to review the preproduction process, such as customer service, artwork, and plate making. Every two hours, representatives from each area reviewed the orders-in-process to determine if they were meeting service levels at each stage. If they were not, they took corrective action by releasing work to the next stage and redeploying resources (workers), as necessary. The review took about five minutes to perform, taking up only 20 minutes per shift—a small price to pay to ensure the company's competitive performance.

LEAN EXAMPLE

The engineering manager at one company wanted to improve flow and reduce lead time of the design process. In the past, the manager would hold meetings every two weeks to determine the status of the various design efforts in process. However, scheduled completion dates continued to slip. To correct this, the manager determined the demand in terms of engineering hours required per period (e.g., per week). Then he broke demand down into blocks of time that related to actual deliverable items, such as engineering drawings. Finally, he established a management timeframe of two days, meaning that each engineer had a specific task assigned that had to be completed in two days. The manager reviewed progress every two days to determine if the engineers were meeting the service level. If not, the manager took corrective action, such as reassigning resources or tasks to keep the value stream performance on track.

Question 7: What Process Improvements Will Be Necessary to Achieve the Future State?

This final question focuses on the actual activities necessary to incorporate all of the design features for the new future state. Achieving each change to the current state requires some form of improvement effort. Examples of these types of improvements at a process level span the gamut of the tools and techniques embedded in the Lean toolbox, such as

- Standardized work
- Changing batch practices
- Layout changes
- Visual controls
- Cross-functional teams
- Error-proofing

The company will also need other efforts for office and service improvements at a system level, which might include

- Creating new performance metrics
- Reorganizing or realigning portions of the office
- Clearly defining customer requirements
- Establishing sequential pull systems

To be clear, the objective of Question 7 is *not to* create a lengthy list of improvements, but rather to identify those necessary to make the envisioned future state a reality, which we'll discuss in Chapter 9. But first, we will create a future state for the Quick Loan Bank case study.

Chapter 8

Quick Loan Bank Future State

To recap, the Quick Loan Bank value mapping team has shared the current state map with others in the organization and incorporated their input. Now they've scheduled another day to create the future state map and apply the future state questions to guide the redesign discussion.

What Does the Customer Really Need?

Several external customer needs were defined during the preparation activity for the value stream mapping effort. First, auto dealers want a one-day turnaround time, which they believe will greatly help their close rates. The future state will be designed with this primary goal in mind. Remember, the current turnaround or lead time from application to notification ranges from 1.4 to 5.6 days, as identified during the creation of the current state map in Chapter 6. The team needs to establish intermittent lead time goals within the value stream to ensure that the one-day objective can be met. The team will also have to look for creative approaches in processing the work to meet this challenge.

To help themselves get their heads and their hands around the future state design, the team identified three "chunks" for the value stream: "Gather Information and Negotiate," "Verify," and "Fund." The team set a goal of one hour for the "Gather Information and Negotiate" chunk. In other words, Quick Loan Bank will review applications, set pricing and terms, communicate these to the customer, and complete any necessary negotiations within one hour of receipt of a loan application. A maximum of four hours is the goal for the "Verify" chunk, and a goal of one hour was established for the "Fund" segment.

To meet these aggressive lead time targets, the team realized it needed to significantly improve the quality of information throughout the value stream. Starting with the information received from the dealers—the beginning of the "Gather Information and Negotiate" chunk—the team members made a quick list of the specific information requirements they would need to process the loan applications. Because the list didn't seem daunting at all, the team set a target of 100% complete and accurate (C&A) for the loan application information received from the dealers. Continuing to the "Verify" chunk, the team made a similar list of information requirements for the contract package received from the dealers. The team set a target of 90% C&A for the contract package, as team members could envision continued difficulties in obtaining a few pieces of information. The contract itself already had a 100% C&A in the

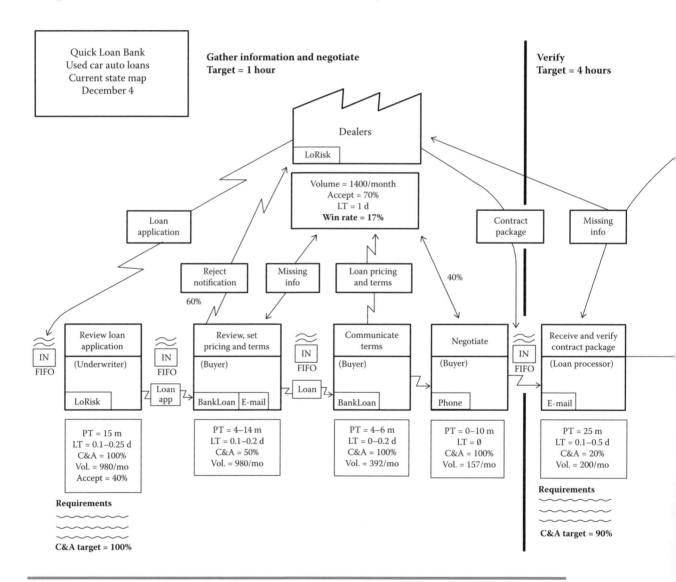

Figure 8.1 (A) Marked-up current state map after Future State Question 1. (*Continued*)

current state when the "Fund" chunk began. The team saw no change in this metric and kept this as a target.

Although the total volume of loan applications is *not* expected to increase, Quick Loan Bank expects that its "win rate" will double from 8.5% to 17% as a result of its improved turnaround time. The increase in win rate will affect processes later in the value stream, specifically in the "Verify" and "Fund" segments. This too will be a consideration in the future state design as management wants to achieve this goal with the same number of Loan Processors that exist today. The team noted all of this information on the current state map, as shown in Figure 8.1.

With these key future state design parameters clearly defined, the team moved on to the next future state question.

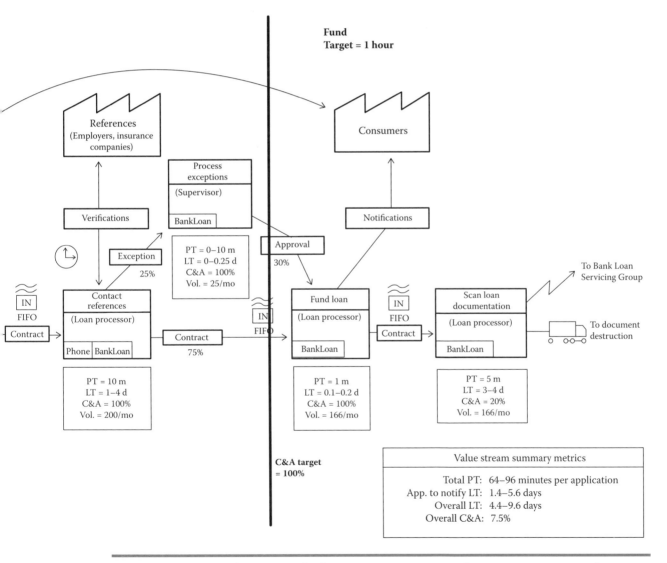

Figure 8.1 (Continued) **(B) Marked-up current state map after Future State Question 1.**

Which Steps Create Value and Which Generate Waste?

The waste that has the most impact on turnaround time is "Correction" waste, as measured by overall C&A for the value stream, estimated in Chapter 6 to be 7.5% for the current state. It is creating waiting waste, as missing and/or correct information is gathered. Further, it requires additional process time for the buyers who reviewed the loan application and set pricing and terms. Clearly, this waste must be addressed if Quick Loan Bank is to meet its one-day turnaround target. The team discussed several ideas, and ultimately agreed to add additional required fields into the LoRisk software program. The fields would prompt the dealers to provide *all* required information before transmitting it to Quick Loan Bank. The C&A measure at the "Review, Set Pricing & Terms" step will increase to near 100% as a result.

Moving on to the "Verify" segment, the team focused on the missing information in the contract package, and the wait time and extra effort associated with it. This is a major source of waste, as the current C&A is 20%. The team agreed that a contract checklist would be designed and sent to the dealer and consumer along with the loan pricing and terms, which is expected to significantly improve the C&A of the contract package.

How Can Work Flow with Fewer Interruptions?

One of the team members then challenged the "Review Loan Application" step currently performed by an underwriter. "Do we really need the underwriters to perform the first review step? The underwriters simply follow some standard guidelines to decide which loan applications to accept and which to reject." The team agreed that the underwriter's "rules" could be embedded in the LoRisk software program. Near-immediate notification of acceptance and rejection could be provided to the dealers and in turn, the customer.

The team consulted with the Information Technology department, who said that the program changes could be made within two months, including the additional required fields and an automated transfer of loan application information from the LoRisk system into the BankLoan system. With this information in hand, the team felt confident including these changes in the future state. The underwriter's involvement in this value stream will be eliminated. By eliminating a handoff between departments, the potential for a queue to form will also be eliminated.

A team member pointed out that the existing queue between "Review, Set Pricing & Terms" and "Communicate Terms" can also be eliminated, given the expected near 100% C&A for the loan application. The buyers would not have to put aside loan applications while they waited for missing information, only to come back to them to complete and then communicate terms to the dealer and consumer. This could all be done in one step.

The team continued to mark up the current state map to reflect the changes proposed (see Figure 8.2). The team was feeling very positive that the one-hour turnaround goal for the "Gather Information and Negotiate" segment of the value stream could be consistently met.

Another idea was to request a copy of a recent paycheck as evidence of employment and income. This would eliminate the need to contact employer references, which was always problematic. For example, employers were not always available on Saturdays, which often required waiting until Monday or even longer to get verification of employment and income. A request for a copy of the paycheck will be included in the contract checklist.

Contacting the insurance company reference can also be eliminated. Part of the service that the dealer provides is to help the consumer arrange for insurance before driving the purchased car off the dealer's lot. Quick Loan Bank would ask the dealer for evidence that the required insurance was in place. This too would be included in the contract checklist. Therefore, loan processors would no longer need to spend an estimated 10 minutes per loan to contact references.

The team projected that the contract package C&A would increase from 20% to 90% (certainly there would still be some issues). They also estimated that as a result of the improved C&A, only half the time, or 12.5 minutes, would be required to review the contract package in the future state. Altogether, the total process time for the loan processors would decrease from 41 minutes to 18.5 minutes per loan, or approximately 55%. Therefore the current staffing level for loan processors could handle the expected twofold increase in volume in the future state.

Another key interruption in flow that still remains involves the processing of exceptions by the supervisor. In the current state, 25% of loans are sent to the supervisors for additional review, of which 30% are approved and sent back to the loan processor. The team agreed that they would increase authority levels for the loan processors, which would reduce the volume going to the supervisor in the future state. They are unable to eliminate this interruption completely, but at least can reduce the frequency that it occurs. Nevertheless, the target of four hours for the "Verify" segment of the value stream now looked easily achievable, with an estimated 83% of the loans being processed in approximately one hour. The other 17% might take another hour or so for the supervisor to review.

The team then moved on to the "Fund" chunk of the value stream. To recall, the target was a one-hour turnaround for the "Fund" segment. Currently, it takes approximately 45 to 90 minutes to fund the loan, plus an additional three to four days to scan the documentation. The loan processors were in no rush to scan the documents and send them to the Bank Loan Servicing Group, though the step took just five minutes. The 45- to 90-minute range in lead time to fund the loan was due primarily to increased volume during busy days. To recall, volumes could almost triple based on the day of the week. The unleveled volume will be addressed in Future State Question 5. As for the delay in scanning, the team agreed that loan processors would immediately scan all documents on funding

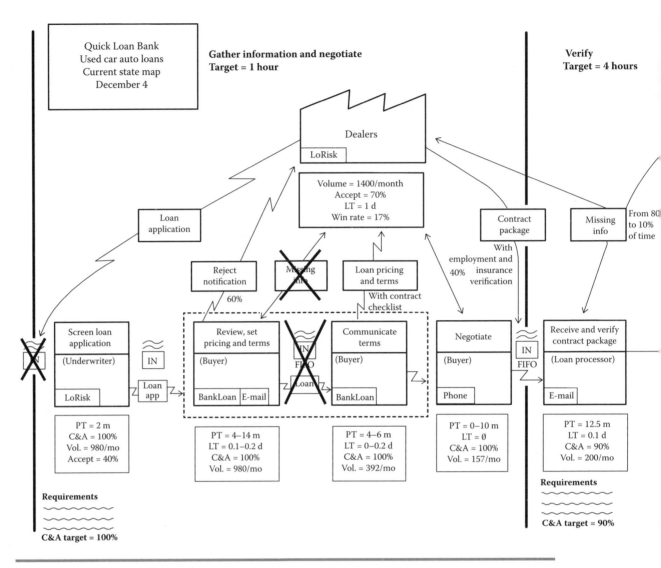

Figure 8.2   (A) Marked-up current state map after Future State Questions 2 and 3.
(Continued)

the loan, rather than putting the documents aside to be scanned later when they were not as busy. This practice would be reflected in the loan processors' new standard work. Given the time savings elsewhere in the value stream, the loan processors agreed that this was possible. The team continued to mark up the current state throughout discussion of Question 3 (see Figure 8.2).

How Will Interruptions in the Flow Be Controlled?

The team reviewed each chunk of the value steam for remaining potential points of interruption in the flow. In the "Gather Information and Negotiate" segment, it is possible that loan applications received into the BankLoan system by way of the LoRisk system could wait for some period of time for a buyer to begin his

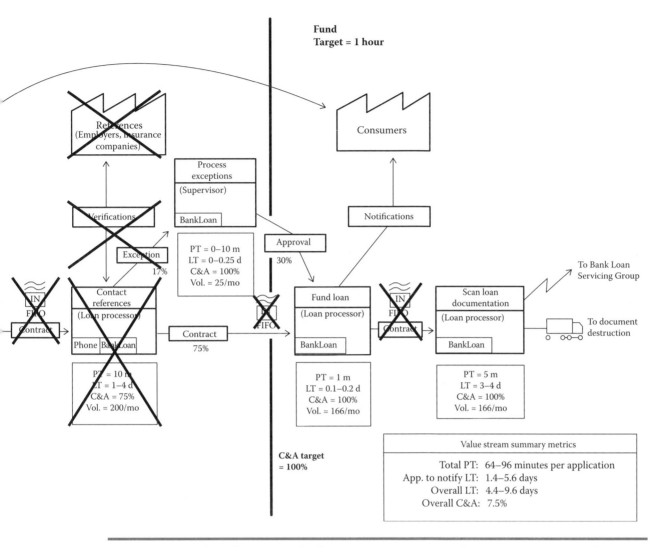

Figure 8.2 (Continued) **(B) Marked-up current state map after Future State Questions 2 and 3.**

or her process? Similarly, contract packages received from dealers could queue up, waiting for a loan processor. The team agreed that if queues did form, it was important to maintain a high service level for "high-priority" dealers. Therefore, these would be processed first rather, than a pure "first-in-first-out" (FIFO) sequence.

In addition, if either interruption was growing too long, say more than one hour, then additional resources would need to be "pulled" to lend support. Specific buyers and loan processors will be identified, cross trained, and given access to all required systems so that they help out when volumes are high or team members are absent. It was agreed that with proper staffing for the "peak periods" the need to "pull" other resources could be minimized. This issue will be discussed during Question 5. Nevertheless, continual visibility of these two important queues will be imperative to maintaining quick turnaround in the future state. Reports from the BankLoan and e-mail systems will be developed

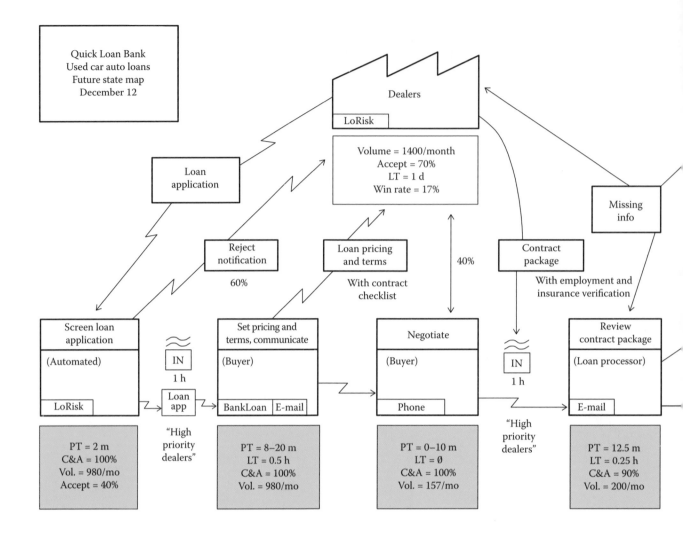

Figure 8.3   (A) Future state map up through Future State Question 4.   (*Continued*)

to identify when loan applications or contracts have been sitting in queue beyond the desired time.

The team members felt that they now could map out the future state incorporating all that has been discussed so far, as seen in Figure 8.3.

How Will the Workload and/or Activities Be Leveled?

As identified during the preparation activity for the value stream mapping exercise, the volume of loan applications varies significantly based on the day of the week. This information was provided in Figure 4.1. In real terms, the number of loan applications can range from 23 to 34 per day on Tuesdays through Fridays, to 60 to 70 on Saturdays and Mondays. The number of loans would vary similarly.

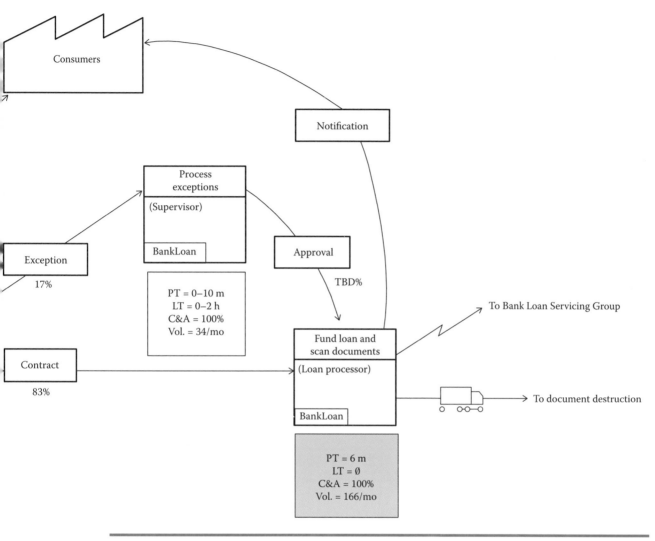

Figure 8.3 (Continued) **(B) Future state map up through Future State Question 4.**

There is nothing that could be done to address the root cause of this variation. Consumers tend to go shopping for used cars on weekends. Therefore, all that Quick Loan Bank can do is staff accordingly. The office will be staffed to match demand from day to day. With the expected new process times, historic loan application volumes, and projected new volume of loans, a staffing plan was easily created for buyers and loan processors (see Appendix II). The challenging part was to present the plan to office personnel to determine how best to make the plan a reality.

How Will We Manage the New Process?

There are two levels of management that the team wants to begin with: the "front line," where the value is created in the loan process and the next level of leadership up in the organization (the supervisor or manager level). Given the targets for short turnaround time, there is a need to review the performance of the value steam frequently so that corrections can be made if necessary, and service levels can be maintained. Establishing a regular "cadence" for this review is important. The team felt that a review every hour would be necessary. The review will be performed by representatives for the buyers and loan processors, who ideally will get together in person. They will review the wait time at the two identified queues using reports that were developed for this purpose. Together they will make decisions on the reallocation of resources if necessary. Other important process metrics will also be reviewed to verify that the value stream is performing as expected. These will be posted visibly in the office so that all team members are aware of them.

In addition, all involved buyers and loan processors will be encouraged to identify any "problem" applications or contracts. These will be escalated to the appropriate supervisor for corrective action and possible process improvement if the team members cannot resolve them themselves. For example, perhaps a particular dealer is not using the contract checklist properly. This will require deliberate follow-up to effect the necessary change in the dealer's behavior. A visual board will be used by team members to identify problems, assign responsibility for follow-up, and provide the status of the ensuing effort.

This first tier or level of process management is a necessary step toward the second level of process management: the first tier of leaders (supervisors or managers) is responsible for solving problems beyond the day-to-day. They have chosen to focus on several metrics, each supporting the organization's overall goals: trends of day-to-day performance, loan win rates, loan volume trends, and productivity trends within the loan process. All of these metrics deal with issues that are outside the control of the value creators: the value creators are focused on getting the work done correctly, not on how things might change over time. Although day-to-day performance can be captured within the first level of process management, win rate and productivity data, for example, don't necessarily come from that first tier.

The first tier of management needs to work with the value-adding team members to determine the best way to create these important metrics. How will the required raw data be captured? How will it be used to generate the higher-level metrics to identify trends over time? Once there is agreement on the processes to capture and generate the metrics, supervisors or managers will post them on the aforementioned visual board. Then *everyone* can see if the changes are producing the long-term results they are seeking. Is the win rate improving as projected? Is productivity where it needs to be as volume is increasing? If the visual metrics are indicating problems (i.e., not meeting goals and expectations), leaders will start to analyze what might be happening from a higher-level perspective (e.g., volumes slipping due to competitive action, turnaround targets not being met due to the impact of new regulations). The "front-line" supervisors or managers will then review these data—let's say weekly—with their leaders, along with ideas to correct the undesirable trends.

What Process Improvements Will Be Necessary to Achieve the Future State?

The team projected new value stream summary metrics for the future state. They also noted on the map the key process improvements agreed on during discussion of the first six future state questions. The proposed future state map is shown in Figure 8.4.

With the proposed future state in hand, the team met with other members of the organization to share their thoughts, solicit input, and in general to get buy-in of the vision and concepts upon which the future state is based. They first met with those whose agreement with the recommendations, at least in principle, was critical to success. This included the supervisors of loan processors, the supervisors of buyers, and the dealers. Next, the team met with those individuals and groups in the organization that needed to accept the changes. This included the buyers and loan processors who were not part of the mapping team. These individuals will be asked to change their current practices and therefore will be directly impacted. Finally, the team made several presentations to those who just needed to be made aware of the changes, as they may be impacted in an indirect way. This included representatives from the loan servicing center.

The team emphasized that the future state is not cast in stone. It is subject to revision as changes are made and the effects of those changes assessed. The team explained that the details of the recommended changes would come later. Various members of the organization would be asked to participate in small-team activities to work those details out and to initiate pilots or experiments to verify that the changes are having the expected benefits. Substantive discussion took place as members of the organization asked important questions of the team. This helped everyone gain a fuller understanding of what was being proposed. After a while, the conversation turned from "what" the recommendations were to "when" they could be implemented. Everyone was very excited about the potential benefits that the future state would bring. The team's next task is to develop an implementation plan to achieve the future state, which we'll discuss in Chapter 9.

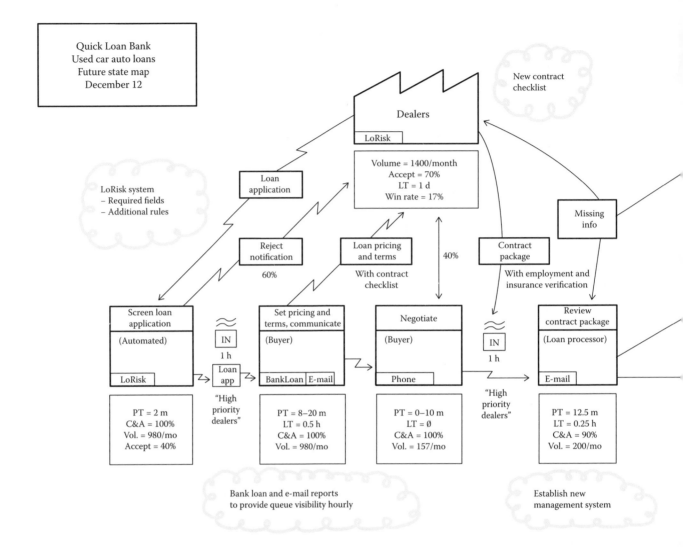

Figure 8.4   **(A) Proposed future state.**   **(Continued)**

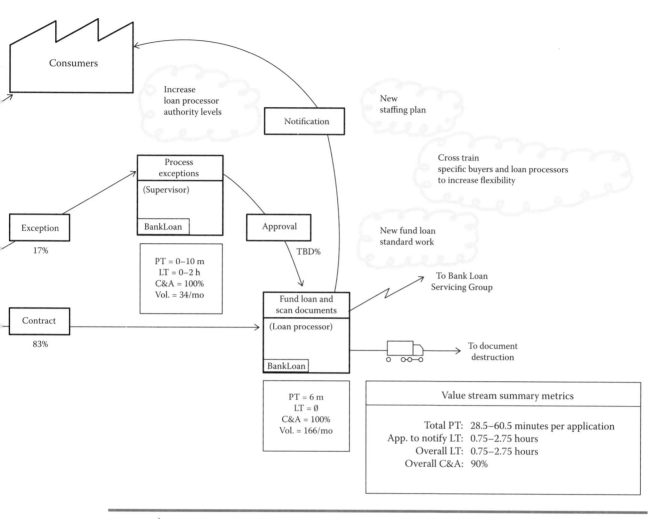

Figure 8.4 (Continued) **(B) Proposed future state.**

Chapter 9

Achieving the Future State

Value stream maps can be very useful tools in designing a new way of doing business, but they represent only the beginning of the Lean journey. To embrace value stream management as a way of doing business, companies must implement the future state maps rapidly within an organization committed to realizing the improvements. There are many ways to go about prioritizing and implementing the changes required by the future state map, and we will certainly make several suggestions later in this chapter. But first, it is necessary to truly understand what the future state represents, as well as the general approach that organizations must take during implementation.

The future state represents a visual hypothesis. The belief at this time is that *if* the new value stream design and the concepts upon which it is based are implemented, it will achieve the objectives defined. But it is just a hypothesis that can be tested only through actual experimentation. The effort to this point gets the team through the "Plan" element of the "Plan–Do–Check–Act" (PDCA) improvement cycle. "Do–Check–Act" is still to come. It is important for organizations to understand that the implementation of the future state is an experiment—a series of experiments, really. The results of these experiments will trigger adjustments to the future state design as the organization learns what is and is not effective. For this reason, the future state map and the accompanying implementation plan must be viewed as working documents that will be updated frequently.

It has been our experience that organizations want a high level of certainty that the future state will perform as projected before they will even take the first step. Often they will develop very detailed plans to implement the envisioned future state, thereby providing some false sense of certainty about how it will all take place. Unfortunately, however, too much will still remain unknown, and such approaches are indicative of a lack of understanding of the objective of Lean thinking itself—to create a culture of continuous improvement that encourages experimentation. Leaders in particular must provide a "safe" environment for the team and the organization overall to perform the necessary experiments. Of course, these experiments should be conducted in "smart" ways to reduce the risk to the organization if undesirable outcomes result. The team must learn, adjust, and move on as it strives to achieve the future state.

There are several critical success factors in achieving a Lean transformation, but three are always at the top of the list:

1. Organizational leaders who understand and embrace Lean concepts, and who stay focused on the business reasons that prompted the value stream redesign
2. Value stream managers who have the authority and time to coordinate and facilitate the implementation, as well as a passion for the cause
3. Appropriate team members who have the time and ability to put toward implementing elements of the future state over time

Tie the Value Stream Design to the Company's Business Objectives

The Lean journey is difficult, especially for mature companies faced with an "anti-Lean" culture with anchor-dragging managers who are antagonistic to the Lean way. It is critically important for everyone to stay focused on the key business reasons for change. It is far too easy after the value stream mapping exercise for everyone to return to their "real jobs" and leave the future state unimplemented in part or even in its entirety. Up to this point, the changes are literally just on paper. During the implementation, existing resistance in the organization will become apparent. Organizational leaders will need to periodically revisit the pressing need for change of the current state. This means that management must focus on making sure its operating strategy (i.e., its future state map) supports its business plan (i.e., the company's strategy). It is imperative for those committed to Lean thinking to stay on message throughout the implementation and turn the early adopters into true believers, who in turn will help win over the more cautious team members.

It has also been our experience that the best approach is to "do a few things and move on." In other words, do not attempt to implement the entire future state en masse. This would undermine the aforementioned spirit of experimentation that is part of every Lean enterprise. The logical next question, then, is "Well, where do we start?" With the operating and business strategy in hand, this question becomes much easier to answer, and logic and reason also have an important part to play. Sometimes it just makes sense to take a particular approach to achieving the future state, but nevertheless, we will provide some general guidelines for you to consider.

Identify "Chunks" in the Future State and Prioritize

Radical changes in the sequencing and timing of activities envisioned in the future state will require more time and experimentation to achieve. To help the team get their heads and hands around what can seem like an impossible undertaking, consider breaking down the future state into segments or "chunks." In Chapter 7, we discussed identifying segments of the value stream. It is often helpful to view the future state once again in this way, to determine an appropriate and viable approach to achieving it. As previously discussed, "chunks" often begin and end at major interfaces in the value stream and often represent segments of flow between these interfaces. It must be restated that the chunks identified when marking up the current state at the beginning of the design of the future state may no longer be appropriate. New ones may need to be identified based on the proposed future state.

Once the chunks are identified, the team can prioritize which chunk it should focus on first, then second, and so on. Entire chunks may be left unaddressed if deemed appropriate. Remember, it is *not* about working on everything, but on the right things. Consideration of the business objectives is key here. For example, if it is necessary to achieve quick improvement in customer service, then priority should be given to the segment of the value stream that has the greatest impact on customer experience.

Develop a Plan to Implement the Envisioned Future State for Each Chunk

Within each chunk, there will be a number of process improvements that must be made to achieve the future state. Once again, some prioritization may help here. Here are a few guidelines that readers may find helpful.

- First, eliminate all non-value-added activities that are able to be eliminated. This sends a quick and powerful message to the organization.
- Second, consider initiating techniques that will improve information and service quality. These include standardized work, checklists, even mistake-proofing techniques that often can be implemented in short timeframes (within three months). The organization can realize important benefits as a result, including improved flow, increased customer satisfaction, and reduced process and lead time.
- Next, simplify any remaining activities that require *minimal* information technology support. Note the term "minimal." These should be changes that can be accomplished in short timeframes (within three months).
- Change the flow of work as envisioned in the future state. This will require a change in roles and responsibilities, *where* particular activities are

Action	Resp.	Jan	Feb	Mar	Apr	May	June
1. Create new contract checklist	R. Smith	⟷					
2. Create new staffing plan	J. Jones	⟷					
3. Buyer, loan processor cross training	A. Burns		⟷				
4. Increase loan processor authority	S. Stevens		⟷				
5. Create new fund loan standard work	R. Smith		⟷				
6. Changes to LoRisk system	A. Techie		⟵——————⟶				
7. Create queue reports	J. Jones			⟷			
8. Establish new management system	J. Jones			⟵————————————⟶			

Figure 9.1   **Quick Loan Bank implementation plan.**

performed, batch practices, work-in-process policies, and the like. Here is where significant resistance can arise. The improvements made leading up to this point will greatly help to increase acceptance by team members of concepts that represent more significant change and will take longer to implement (three to six months).

■ Finally, implement the solutions requiring significant information technology support, and are truly necessary to achieve the future state.

Using these guidelines will help the mapping team focus on simplifying activities and eliminating waste before using and/or investing in technology. It has been our experience that there is a tendency for value stream mapping teams to assume new or significantly revised information technology systems and tools as part of the future state design. This substantially extends the time to implement the future state (six to twelve months or longer), and can significantly decrease the probability for success. "Creativity before capital" is a theme that should be considered throughout the future state design and development of the implementation plan. An implementation plan for the Quick Loan Bank future state may look something like what is shown in Figure 9.1.

Sharing with the Organization

Once the implementation plan has been created, it too must be shared with the organization. Effectively socializing the plan is critical to success. In particular, it must be shared with those people and departments who are part of the current state and who will be affected by the changes envisioned by the future state map—those who must agree or accept the changes to be made. They must be made aware of what is coming and when. The implementation itself will provide an opportunity for others in the organization to get more involved in the effort. Specific members may be asked to join teams responsible for implementing specific identified improvements.

Note that this represents the *beginning* of the socialization process, and that frequent updates must be provided. Posting the maps and the plan at appropriate locations in the organization can really help communication throughout the implementation process. It can also generate much–needed dialogue as the team engages other members of the organization to determine the best way to achieve the future state.

LEAN NOTE

Too often the important documents created during the value stream mapping exercise and the information that they contain are *not* adequately shared with others in the organization beyond the team and senior management. This is a missed opportunity to share the substantial learning that the value stream mapping team experienced during the exercise and seek feedback from other perspectives. In addition, it is a common cause for problematic implementation, as members of the organization remain unaware of the vision and the plan. Sometimes the documents are transferred to an electronic medium with the false hope that people will make the effort to seek them out and periodically review them. There is no substitute for simply posting the documents, including the maps, in visible locations in the organization, and taking the time to periodically review and/or request feedback from all team members.

Let the Experiments Begin!

To ensure success, the team will meet regularly with the value stream manager, typically every week or every other week. The meetings should take place not just in conference rooms, but also at appropriate points of the value stream where changes have been made. The results of any experiments, as well as any obstacles encountered, will be shared at these meetings, and adjustments to the future state map and the plan will be made accordingly. The value stream manager will "escalate" all significant obstacles to senior leadership for resolution as they become identified. In addition, senior management should review the plan and the progress made to date on a regular basis, typically monthly throughout the implementation. The value stream manager, with the support of the team, will facilitate these reviews.

Achieving the future state is where the rubber hits the road—the "Do–Check–Act" of the PDCA improvement cycle. Several of the process improvements will be of the "just do it" variety, simple efforts that can be accomplished quickly with modest effort. Even "just do it" type changes should be considered experiments, the effects of which must be verified. Others will lend themselves to a highly focused rapid improvement approach also called a "kaizen event." This approach is highly effective for conducting rapid PDCA cycles for specific concepts that are part of the future state design. There is a bias during these events for "trystorming"—to put ideas into action to learn what is effective and what is not, the true essence of experimentation. The progress that the team ultimately makes in achieving the future state will depend on the frequency and effectiveness of these learning cycles. Kaizen events are also highly motivational because people can see that change can occur quickly, and they are directly involved in it. Standardized work, visual management techniques, office layout changes, sequential pull systems, mistake-proofing devices, and other concepts can typically be created and tested during multiday kaizen events. Reference to the future state map should be made on every occasion as changes are made by whatever means.

Other process improvements will require more time to implement as they represent change of a larger scope and scale. Often, these involve changes to existing or the creation of new information technology systems and tools. In such cases, opportunities to experiment on elements of these improvements at various stages of their development must always be sought. For example, mockups of screen designs can be demonstrated before actual programming begins. Specific program functions can be tested as they become available. Perhaps it is a change in policy. It would be prudent to test the new policy on a limited basis to determine its effect. That way, any necessary alterations to the policy can be made before rolling it out. The iterative nature of these experiments is depicted in Figure 9.2.

We've learned that a combination of these approaches will be needed to achieve the future state successfully. In all cases, each experiment on the work process will follow its own PDCA cycle. The value stream mapping team, or a different team identified specifically for this purpose, will take an idea for the future state and *plan* the experiment. This involves clearly defining the target or objective of the experiment, which should be specific and measurable when

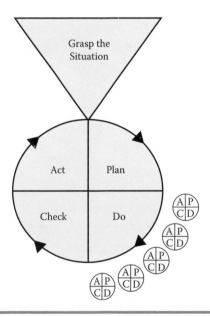

Figure 9.2 Multiple PDCA cycles during the "Do" stage.

possible. The team will want to understand more fully the current situation in the area that the experiment will take place. A more thorough observation of the specific process that will be changed should be conducted—far beyond what was done during the value stream mapping exercise. Additional data may be collected from the process for this purpose.

With this deeper understanding of the process, the team can identify specific potential obstacles and select an obstacle or several to address during the experiment. The key here is to *not* select too many obstacles to address at the same time, as this can make the experiment difficult to conduct and the results of the experiment difficult to interpret. The team can also obtain greater acceptance from the people who will be part of the experiment by keeping the experiments narrow in scope.

Specific changes to be made are agreed on and steps to affect them are determined as the team prepares to *do* the experiment. Steps to mitigate the risk of any negative effects of the experiment can also be taken. This is part of providing a "safe" environment for experimentation, to give people confidence to go forward with the changes to the work process. For example, proposed changes to a computer software program may be made in a test environment developed for this purpose while everyone else in the office continues to work in the regular production environment. Once the changes have proven to work to everyone's satisfaction, the new program can be released for everyone's use. Most all changes can be made in safe ways. Let's say that the change involves a person assuming new responsibilities, perhaps to eliminate a handoff. The team can select a single person to serve as the subject of the experiment. A decision to roll out the change to others will be made only after sufficient time has passed to *check* if the experiment is working as hypothesized. The roll-out and all that is involved with it (e.g., updating procedures, providing training) *act* to make the proven change the new standard. With this as a backdrop, we will now have an expanded discussion of each component of PDCA for a specific experiment as we "learn our way to the future state."

Plan

Here are some good design questions to work through when designing the "Plan." The overriding conceptual questions that drive the theme of the experiment design include

- How can it be "small and reversible"?
- How quickly can we learn and adjust?
- What risks do we need to avoid (and how will we do it)?
- How can we engage the minds of people who live within the scope of the experiment?
- How do we create and ensure a "safe zone" where people can try new ideas without fear of retribution if the ideas don't have the effect expected?

The tactical questions the design team should consider include

- What should we measure to evaluate the changes? What is our baseline performance? (Note: This needs to be established prior to running the experiment.)
- What specific changes will be made?
- Who will be involved, what will be their new tasks (e.g., standard)?
- When will it occur and for how long?
- How will we collect the data in terms of the data source, frequency of measurement, and duration of measurement?
- Who will check the data and how often?
- How will we structure and socialize your design?
- How will we get feedback during and after the pilot?
- How will we discuss and socialize the results?
- What visuals will we use to assist in the socialization process?
- How will we plan for "abnormal" situations that may arise? When a "problem" surfaces: Who logs the problem? Who responds? How does he or she know to respond?

We've seen great designs include a concept called "progressive experiments." This means that the experiment starts small and builds upon itself to encompass a broader scope. As an example, an accounting department wanted to change the way it interacted with field offices during the month-end close. The staff chose to start with just a few specific transactions with a few specific offices, and used these early experiments to "shake out" the work to make it technically and socially compatible. They then progressed by adding more types of transactions and offices for the next month-end close, making further adjustments and continuing this process until all field offices and transactions were covered. This "progressive experiment" not only allowed the ability to learn from small, less risky changes, but also included the specific engagement of a growing number of field office employees. By the time the experiment was concluded, nearly everyone was engaged and involved in the technical and social changes necessary for the organization to succeed!

Do

Although this PDCA component might seem obvious, let's cover a few things to minimize interruptions in the experiment:

- Before running the experiment, consider completing a dry run to adjust the procedures for the experiment, as well as the procedures for observing the experiment and collecting data.
- Socialize the experiment with others who will be involved in it by sharing the design and inviting their input.

- For those not directly involved, develop a "thumbnail sketch" of the experiment (purpose, timing, goals) to inform everyone who needs to know.
- As the experiment is being conducted, interview the participants and get their feedback: this social engagement has proven to be as important as the metrics in terms of creating a successful work redesign.

Check

This is what many teams forget to do, and represents critical scientific thinking: Did we achieve what we wanted to achieve? And if not, why not? Remembering that we want both technical and social changes to occur, we need to make sure that the metrics, behaviors, and thinking are all in synch with each other. It's time to take a look at the performance metrics and huddle with the participants to get their feedback. It is important to look *and* listen to gain valuable information on the effects of the experiment.

Act/Adjust

If you haven't achieved what you want to achieve, consider these options:

- Modify the experiment and try again under the same or similar circumstances.
- Repeat the experiment in slightly different circumstances (e.g., a different group of people, different shift, or different location).
- Scrap the existing experiment and try a new approach.

This should *not* be viewed as a failure. As long as the team learns from the experience and continues to press on then progress is being made.

If you have achieved what you want to achieve, then conclude the experiment and document the new standard work reflecting the experimental work design. Instruct all individuals involved in the new standard. Leaders must remember that continual reinforcement will be necessary until the new standard becomes the new habit.

LEAN EXAMPLE

As a result of a value stream mapping effort, a company identified a radically different approach to its order process. In the current state, the order passed through five different departments over an average of three days. The value stream mapping team believed that four of those steps could be consolidated to one person and that a two-person team working together could process orders more effectively and efficiently. They hypothesized that the time to process orders could be reduced to a half day *and* that the orders processed per person—a measure of productivity— would *increase*. There was strong skepticism among members of the organization that the latter would be the case. Therefore, the team set up two teams for the experiment involving four people out of an office of 36 associates. New standard work was created and training provided to the four people. The experiment was conducted for *three* months, during which adjustments were made to the approach based on what the team learned. The experiment continued until important process data demonstrated that the approach was effective. At that time, the concept was expanded to involve the entire office, ultimately resulting in 12 two-person teams. A consistent lead time of a half day was achieved, as well as a productivity improvement of 30%. A 20% reduction in order errors was also a benefit, as the two people responsible for a particular order have a more thorough understanding of the customer's needs. This was very important in this "design-to-order" company.

Leaders have an important role in all of this. They must be supportive without taking over the process. They must provide the aforementioned "safe" environment. Management has an obligation to provide an atmosphere where it is safe for teams to fail as long as said teams learn from the experience and take what they learn to continue the experimentation. In fact, leaders must change the very manner by which they lead—no small task indeed. The role of leaders is explored in depth in the next chapter.

Chapter 10

Leading in the Future State

More and more organizations are using value stream mapping to redesign key business processes and even entire enterprises. However, we've found that they have *not* changed the manner by which those processes or organizations are *managed*, which means that the benefits will be fewer than expected, and even short lived. The need to reconsider traditional management approaches was prompted during discussions of the sixth future state question, "How will the new process be managed?" introduced in Chapter 7. In this chapter, we cover this important topic in depth.

The "work process" and the "management process" are intertwined and synergistic. If the focus is simply on changing the work and ignoring the manner by which the work will be managed, we create an imbalance in the system where there needs to be a synergy. In these instances, organizations have two implicit choices: either change the management of the processes or wait for the work processes to revert back to the legacy system—which might take only a few months. The existing management process acts as a strong "anchor" for the status quo, as depicted in Figure 10.1.

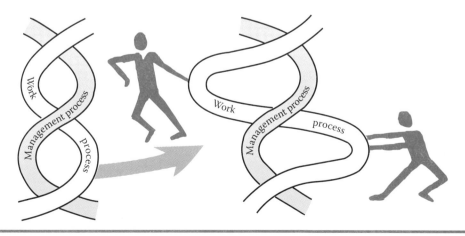

Figure 10.1   **Work process and management process.**

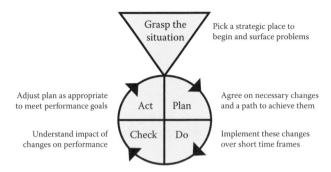

Figure 10.2 PDCA as applied to the management system.

If you would rather sustain the work process improvements, and even further improve on them, then it's time to put the management process, or what we typically refer to as the management *system*, on its own *Plan–Do–Check–Act* (PDCA) cycle! The management system is indeed a process of learning and improving, as depicted in Figure 10.2.

Let's begin with discussing a new way to manage. Imbedded in this new management system are new roles and responsibilities for management, which involve *creating a fundamentally different way to engage with all associates.* Most organizations have a good dose of fear in their culture, primarily the fear of failure. If someone fails at a task or project he or she is generally met with implicit or explicit punitive action. This fear creates an aversion to change and avoidance of big goals. And this can spell disaster for the successful transformation to the future state, which typically represents significant, even radical change. We need everyone to think about focusing on and attending to big goals! The new management system needs to create a "cultural safe zone" where employees can address their problems and discuss and experiment with new ideas. These ideas may or may not work at first, but the result is that the organization is building its "thinking muscle" in a way that will change the culture and lead it to accept some risk in meeting critical goals.

In traditional management systems, we frequently see leadership making all sorts of decisions—some important, some minor—and thereby doing the thinking for the rest of the organization. In one instance, we saw the president of the organization dictating how many people within each function would be optimal for an experiment needed for the future state, but this president was five levels away from the where the work was performed and had yet to observe the work! The rationale was "I've been in this industry for 20 years and I know what is right." Although this example is indeed extreme, it illustrates how often leaders might make decisions for work that is really someone else's.

CULTURE EXAMPLE

One healthcare organization was attempting to create a different management system and found many people coming to a senior leader with suggestions of what they would like to try. After listening to their ideas, he would frequently make additional suggestions ("sounds good….maybe you should also consider…."). He soon noticed that their energy levels dropped when he made suggestions, as they felt compelled to do what the boss suggested as opposed to trying some of their own thinking. He recognized the need to lead in a different manner. He needed to be more of a coach who asks open-ended questions and practice "humble inquiry" (more about this later).

We've learned over the years that leaders have an explicit role in challenging the culture and status quo to develop an organization of engaged problem solvers. People in this new management system understand

■ What problems are their specific responsibility to solve
■ How to identify, understand, and communicate the problems and opportunities they face
■ How to engage in experimentation to learn the best way to meet the goals set forth by the organization
■ How to socialize and engage others in their thinking and acting so that solutions are not created in isolation

As the organization moves toward this model, the focus is much more on *becoming Lean* than *doing Lean*. None of this is possible without unending engagement by leaders and a commitment to continue to develop their organizations' problem-solving muscle. However, most organizations aren't at that point yet. Our focus in this regard is to help you understand how to start a new way of thinking and managing. Once you start this effort, your learning will allow you to figure out the best way to proceed as an organization and culture to *become Lean*.

The best way we've found to start on this path is to practice and learn through PDCA, which is implicitly a learning model. So, we're returning to PDCA to show you a way that you can begin this important work of *becoming Lean*. Let's discuss this management PDCA model in more detail.

Using the PDCA Model

Provide Direction

Leaders must establish and communicate a direction for the organization to which significant improvement initiatives, such as the redesign of entire value streams, can be aligned. This direction is typically in the form of a vision. In other words, what *can be*? As leaders begin to create a new management system, they also need to develop a vision of the desired culture and a compelling case for change. Challenges can also be defined—specific goals or milestones along the path toward the vision.

Grasping the Current Situation

At this point, the management team should be assessing its improvement efforts and working to understand what it will take to pilot a new process. Understanding the team dynamics, the culture, and the areas where experiments will be run is critical in figuring out a new process to support and sustain change.

As you consider the culture created by existing management practices some things to discuss include

- What gaps do you see in management or culture that prevent you from moving forward toward the defined vision?
- What should you be most concerned about in managing the changes required in the envisioned future state?
- How would you define success in a new management system to reflect the established direction and existing challenges?

EXAMPLES OF MANAGEMENT SYSTEM CURRENT SITUATIONS

A well-known bank had difficulty getting team leaders to step beyond their day-to-day responsibilities and accountabilities and focus on improving processes and performance. This was identified as an initial need for the new management system, and the bank went on to plan a way for management to coach (as opposed to just providing training) the team leaders to close this gap.

An insurance company had a culture in which the managers did much of the work during peak volumes, which resulted in tenuous situations for the front line value-adding associates. For instance, during peak volume times, team members didn't—or perceived that they didn't—have an equal say as the manager, though everyone was doing the same work. Rather, they ceded responsibility for the front-line problem solving to the managers. This led to the front line waiting for management to make decisions at ALL times, not just during peak times. Fortunately, leadership recognized the need to create distinctive relationships and accountability for the managers and put together a plan to coach both managers and the front line to clearly define boundaries and accountabilities during peak and normal volume times.

In the engineering department of a global company, supervisors and managers believed that "every project is different." The culture was one of perpetual "fire-fighting," and the organization was having difficulty identifying recurring process problems. This was a gap that would require deliberate coaching by leaders to develop, over time, the process improvement skills of the front line supervisors and managers, and in time to help them become process thinkers.

Planning the Change (the "P" in the PDCA Cycle)

The changes in your management system will also be experiments, as we probably can't just flip a switch to make a successful change. Moving into new ways of managing is a big step, full of many surprises. So, as you embark on this new way of thinking and acting as a management team, it's time to be deliberate about how to approach this, in the same way as the teams think about experiments in changing the work process. Several things to consider (and socialize within the organization) for a new management process are

- *Why are we going to try a new management system?* Making a change to the management system implies that keeping it the same would be a problem. What problem do we want to solve? What is the specific purpose of this change that we will communicate to our employees? The answers to this question should draw on the agreed-on long-term direction and vision.
- *What changes are we going to try?* There are many variations on management systems. Some organizations want to manage the performance of a horizontal value stream across departments, or "functional silos," while others want to specifically get many people involved in experiments. Others want to focus on improving accountability first, and then reassess their processes as they move on. The important point is "trying" as opposed to "deciding." It's OK to modify anything you try to make it work within your organization's context.
- *Who will be involved?* A new management system involves several tiers or levels of management. How many levels, and managers, will be involved? This discussion should center on the scope of the experiments required to make the envisioned future state a reality. At what particular points of the value stream will the experiments be conducted? What managers will be involved? Some organizations begin with supervisory levels of management, while others include levels higher up in the organization. This is a multitiered question; remember, the best PDCA involves multiple levels of an organization (we'll discuss this more a bit later in this chapter).
- *When will we do it?* This is, in effect, a series of experiments and it needs a start and stop point to assess the process and make adjustments. Try to think of it in terms of aligning with the future state pilots (or shortly after their initiation). Your ultimate goal, though, is to continue to evolve the system into something that makes sense in the long term.
- *How will we know if it's working?* Knowing how the management pilot is performing is a must in terms of learning and adjusting the process to meet your organizational needs. What will you measure to see if it's meeting its purpose? Employee satisfaction? Employee engagement? Management engagement?
- *How often will you check and adjust?* The decision is yours, but it would be best to do this several times within the timeframe of the work process

experiments. For instance, if the experiments are scheduled to run over three months, it might be useful to check and adjust every month. This way, you can "learn your way" to a new management system in tandem with the front line learning its way to the future state.

■ *Where will we manage it?* This is tightly linked to "who will be involved." Which points of the value stream will be closely monitored by way of periodic "checks?" These points will also be where management coaching will occur via two-way communication processes, also called "huddles," between managers and team members. Typically these interactions take place around visual management systems designed for this purpose.

Starting the New Management System (the "Do" of PDCA)

This portion of PDCA is simply implementing the plan you just developed and measuring the impact of the design. The process is similar to what we've found helpful in work process experiments:

■ Perform a dry run to test the design and make any necessary *adjustments*
■ Create a short introduction of your "new standard" for the teams to clarify what you are learning to do and its purpose
■ Run the huddle and solicit feedback from the participants: how did they feel, what would they suggest changing (timing, content, agenda, interactions, etc.), in the next review

Checking the New Management System (the "C" in PDCA)

Checking the effectiveness of the management interaction and intervention is intended to be a quick reflection and debrief on the activity. Questions and discussions typically revolve around:

■ What did we plan to occur vs. what actually occurred (and why)?
■ What seemed to work well and what didn't seem to work well (and why)?
■ What did we see? This can be both technical (what's happening to the performance?) and social (how is the performance improving, how is the team acting?).
■ What is out of scope of the team's efforts that is adversely affecting them and what should we do about it?
■ Is the work progressing in a way that is still aligned with the problems we want to solve in the organization?
■ How did we respond to the problems the team addressed? This question is critical to ask in the debrief, as it gauges management's ability to hold the team accountable for solving the problems they are uncovering. A good way to have this discussion is around the specific questions management asked the team: How many were closed-ended (and why), how many were

open-ended (and why), and what was the reaction of the team during these questions? And, ultimately, what do we think about all of the questions and are they effective in imparting the proper mindset for problem-solving and process improvement?

■ What was the team members' response? Did they appear to still own the problem? How are they thinking about countermeasures? What are our concerns about their actions/performance/countermeasures?
■ What are they learning and how are they learning it?
■ What have we learned about our management system design?
■ What do we need to learn more about to improve our design (and coaching)?

Acting/Adjusting the Management System (the "A" in PDCA)

This value stream management path is likely new to everyone, and adjustments could come fast and furious as you modify your initial plan to one that works within the context of the work and the organization's emerging new culture. Depending on what the discussions during the "check" section of the PDCA cycle are, options in "adjust" could include

■ Modifying any portion of the current plan
■ Rethinking the questions and ways to improve on humble inquiry
■ Creating action plans to support out-of-scope barriers
■ Agreeing on follow-up coaching for specific concerns and observations

Once this is done, another iteration of PDCA now begins! Of course, management will want to standardize those practices that have proven to be effective. In other words, management will "act" to make them standard. But this will probably occur only after several PDCA "adjust" cycles.

MANAGEMENT SYSTEM PDCA EXAMPLE

A healthcare organization redesigned patient care in several different areas of the hospital and decided to have the new management system be a "team effort," which included all of the hospital's vice presidents. The vice presidents decided to visit one area per week to review the visual management systems that were set up and to engage the value-adding team members. To prepare, they met 30 minutes ahead of the visit to plan the review. They discussed the outcome of the previous visit to the designated care area, and then decided what to discuss during the visit and how to approach it. They even discussed which vice president would ask what question! They then proceeded to the review, interacted with the team members based on what they saw from the various elements of the visual management system, and debriefed the effort as a team. If they thought they should make changes to their plan, they incorporated the changes during this debrief. What a great example of a complete management PDCA cycle!

The Role of Leader Standard Work

Leader standard work is a tool that, if properly applied, can help leaders engage the organization differently until the new way of managing becomes habit and occurs more naturally. Leader standard work encompasses the "how" to lead. It defines the processes, routines, and cadence that leaders go through to check on team and individual problem solving, as well as improvements in performance. The routines are most effective when they take place around visual management devices that have been created specifically for this purpose (we'll talk about that a little later in this chapter). These processes and routines are designed to

- Understand where things stand in the processes
- Understand how people are thinking and acting to improve value stream performance
- Provide and facilitate coaching opportunities to strengthen employees' problem-solving muscles

Leader standard work can't exist without the inherent learning cycles of PDCA imbedded within the process. A leader's standard work will be revised to reflect the approaches in the management system that are proven to be most effective. As we continue to improve on this process, we are developing solid problem-solving capabilities within the organization and enhancing the ability of the organization to adapt quickly to changing conditions.

Building the Thinking Muscles through Humble Inquiry

What we have discussed so far must be done in such a way to be maximally effective and to minimize strong resistance among members in the organization. This approach can be described as "humble inquiry." All of us were probably trained to solve problems quickly, regardless of where they are in the organization. As managers, we are drawn to all of the process-level problems and believe that we are smart enough to help others mired in the front-line problems. The only people smart enough to figure things out are the managers, right?

Not only is this implicitly wrong, but it also creates a cultural dependency on having *all* problems solved by management. The world and its incumbent problems are too complex for a few well-intentioned managers to solve. Our experience and counsel revolves around letting everyone solve the problems they live with: they need to be accountable for thinking and acting differently. One of the key elements in this cultural shift is the use of open-ended questions and humble inquiry in the problem-solving interchanges.

Let's discuss closed-ended versus open-ended questions. Closed-ended questions require a yes/no answer (e.g., "Did the data tell you what you needed to know?") and don't allow much dialogue about the situation. It's hard to develop people's new thinking if they just answer "yes" or "no" whenever you engage them! Open-ended questions are those that cannot be answered with simple yes/no responses. They require more thoughtful and thorough responses, and usually invite a dialogue where the thinking of the other person can be understood and discussed (e.g., "What did you learn from the data?"). And, open-ended questions also serve to keep the other person owning the problems! Humble inquiry demonstrates respect for the other person's ability to think and solve problems. It is best described in Edgar Schein's book *Helping*, which we suggest as a reference on the subject.

The main objective for leaders is to *not* own the problems that can best be solved by team members. Further, leaders cannot own the thinking by providing their ideas and biases. Too often, team members will do what the boss wants to do, and not what they believe is appropriate. The danger here is that team members will relinquish their responsibilities with regard to problem solving and process improvement. If the leader's ideas and direction don't work, the team's response might easily be: "I was just doing what my boss told me to do." Management has taken the responsibility and accountability for solving problems from the team.

To engage others in the responsibility of solving problems, there are a few things to keep in mind (with examples):

If you answer their questions, you now own the problem.
  – Someone approaches you with a problem and asks "What do you think we should do?" If you answer this directly, the solution is yours, not the person's. An open-ended response might be "What do you need to know about this problem to understand it better?"
If you analyze the data, you now own the problem.
  – Once you say something like "Why don't you give me the data?" the accountability for solving the problem has passed to you. As an alternative, humble inquiry might begin with "What are the data telling you, and where is this leading you?" which keeps the thinking at the right level.
If you direct or correct, you now own the problem.
  – Comments like "That's not a good place to start" or "You should go ask [fill in any name] what's going on" now changes the path of their problem solving. As an alternative, humble inquiry might begin with something like "What's your thinking on your scope beginning where it does?" or "What do you know of other departments' perspectives?" which once again keeps the thinking with the person who should be solving the problem.
If you suggest ideas to his/her idea, you now own the problem.
  – It's easy to add to other people's ideas, for example, "That's a good start. Why don't you also look at the variation in the ways different field offices process the information?" And although "Why don't you also measure XXX while you're at it?" may or may not be a good idea, it certainly shouldn't

come from you unless you want to own the problem! A more humble inquiry might be "What are your thoughts in expanding the scope into other areas?" or "What are your assumptions in selecting these metrics?"

The power of humble inquiry is the development of deeper thinking and the accountability to learn about and solve problems at the appropriate level of the organization.

Visual Management: Creating a Focal Point for the Management System

Visual management is a great tool, but it takes a combination of a great management system (as we just discussed) and great visual information to create a focal point for discussion, problem solving, and coaching. Otherwise, visual management becomes passive "wallpaper" rather than an active system to lead and improve through team member engagement. Visual management done right includes data, analysis, and the communication of key information, all of which is easy to see (meaning, not hidden on a computer's hard drive!), and is worker managed. This system should be capable of communicating the following types of information at a glance:

■ How the process is performing
■ Abnormal performance conditions
■ Analysis of abnormal conditions to identify possible root causes so that effective countermeasures can be identified to bring the process back into planned performance parameters
■ The progress of current problem solving and process improvement efforts
■ How those efforts are aligned with higher-level strategies

Although many organizations have implemented some sort of visual information by now, there still remains a gap in understanding that visual management systems (VMSs) are required throughout the organization to provide a focal point to foster discussion of different problems—and their solutions—by groups of appropriate individuals. For purposes of visual management, we call these points of interaction *tiers*. Each tier will have a VMS that will be used to facilitate the necessary discussion.

Front-line supervisors or managers will meet with their teams around a system (Tier 1) designed for their purpose, the content of which is maintained by the team members themselves. Often this occurs during the aforementioned *huddles* scheduled daily at specific times. Goals for the day, current performance, recent issues that have arisen, improvement efforts, and the like are discussed during these huddles. Front-line leaders will provide necessary coaching to their team members during the interactions (more on coaching later in this chapter). Front-line supervisors and managers will meet with their appropriate leaders around a system (Tier 2) designed for their purpose, the content of which is maintained by the front-line leaders themselves. Typically they will meet daily to review performance and discuss outstanding issues that are cross-functional in nature as well as improvement efforts and other topics. Coaching is provided to the front-line leaders by their next level of supervision during the interactions. Those leaders will meet with their next level around the Tier 3 VMS designed for their purpose. Overall performance, upcoming business needs, issues requiring attention of senior leaders, and status of major improvement initiatives are several of the topics covered. And of course, coaching is once again provided. The tiered visual management system is depicted in Figure 10.3. A comprehensive VMS is used to facilitate social interactions at each tier that provide other benefits as well. These include collaboration between functions and departments, a sense of belonging of all team members, and a means to create an environment of trust. The most effective visual management systems have linkages between the tiers to demonstrate the impact of performance and how it aligns to key components of the organization's strategy. This is discussed later in this chapter.

Another critical part of the management system is understanding the need for and purpose of two types of visual data: in-process and outcomes/results. Although everyone is interested in results, we rarely have the ability to improve them until we understand what influences a result. For instance, in healthcare the ability of a clinic to stay on schedule and see all of its patients at the appointed time depends on the completeness and accuracy (C&A) of information about the patient before the physician enters the exam room. If the physician doesn't have complete and accurate information, then the on-time performance is at risk because of the delays incurred while he or she looks for critical information. In this case, we can't improve on-time performance without improving the quality of the information presented to the physician at the time of the appointment.

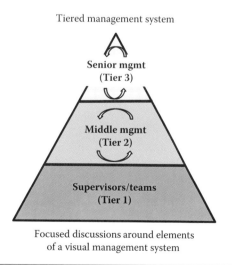

Figure 10.3 Tiered visual management systems.

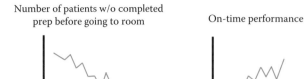

Figure 10.4   **In-process C&A and on-time performance outcome metrics.**

The quality of the information is considered an "in-process" metric that we can measure and improve. And, if we do this the ability to meet on-time performance (our Outcome/Result) is improved. This example is shown in Figure 10.4.

As you think about the processes that you want to improve, what are the "results" you seek, and what factors within the process influence the ability to achieve those results? Once you discuss your thoughts with your team, you'll have a good starting point regarding what to visualize and manage. Every process has in-process and results or outcomes metrics. We need to understand and visualize both. We'll demonstrate this with a few examples (Box 10.1).

Together both types of metrics provide an indication of the "health" of a process. In-process metrics can identify when abnormal conditions occur that will ultimately affect process outcomes. When necessary, corrective action can be

---

BOX 10.1   EXAMPLES OF OUTCOME METRICS VERSUS IN-PROCESS METRICS

- Reducing length of stay (an outcome metric) might be dependent on the ability of a cross-functional staff to efficiently discharge patients on the day they are clinically able to go home (an in-process metric).
- Reducing overtime on month-end closes (outcome metric) might be dependent on the ability to minimize transaction exceptions from field offices (in-process metric).
- Creating a great experience in a restaurant (outcome metric) might be dependent on the consistency of the entrée temperature when served at the table (in-process metric).
- Creating a satisfactory hotel stay (outcome metric) might be dependent on making sure that wake up calls are always made (in-process metric).
- Getting more clients at an new venture group (outcome metric) might depend on getting better information up front to accomplish due diligence (in-process metric).

Please note: *these examples are for illustration purposes only.* We aren't recommending these metrics for you, as all processes, experiments, and metrics are locally driven within the context of your specific organization and business.

taken to reduce the impact on performance of the process, or possibly even to avoid any negative effects altogether. Outcome or results metrics can provide an indication of the impact of changes made to improve the process.

In addition to metrics, the visual management system should include other information that conveys the status of improvement efforts taken or still to come. "Storyboards" are a proven effective way to do this. Storyboards such as "A3s" succinctly describe improvement efforts using PDCA as a framework to do so. An example of a storyboard is provided in Figure 10.5.

The various visual management systems provide a focal point for discussions between leaders at different tiers. Status, obstacles, and results can be communicated from Tier 1 to Tier 2 and 3 leaders during regular visits to the tier 1 leader's area of responsibility. During these interactions, Tier 2 leaders can provide coaching as necessary to Tier 1 leaders. Most important is coaching to develop the problem-solving and process improvement skills of the lower-tier leaders. In addition, these exchanges provide opportunities for senior leaders to reinforce the strategy and direction of the organization, to maintain awareness of what is actually happening, and to develop an environment of trust. All of this can be repeated during regular interactions between Tier 2 and Tier 3 leaders at the Tier 2 visual management system. Tier 3 leaders can provide coaching as necessary to Tier 2 leaders.

Tier 3 leaders can also serve a "second coaching" role to Tier 2 leaders, and Tier 2 leaders can do the same for Tier 1 leaders. For example, a senior leader can periodically observe the Tier 2 leader interacting with their team members or peers. If undesirable behavior is being demonstrated, the senior leader can provide feedback and guidance to the Tier 2 leader to correct it. Of course, these discussions must always remain respectful. Similarly, Tier 2 leaders can observe Tier 1 leaders interacting with their team members. Once again, coaching can be provided as necessary. Such "second coaching" can be very important in the

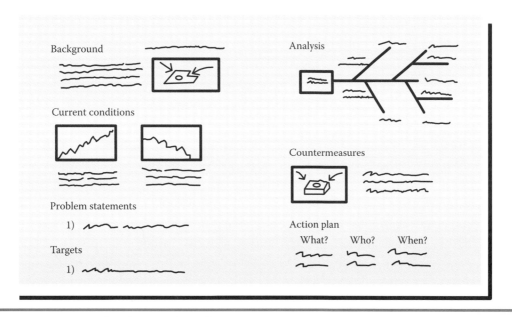

Figure 10.5   **Example of a storyboard.**

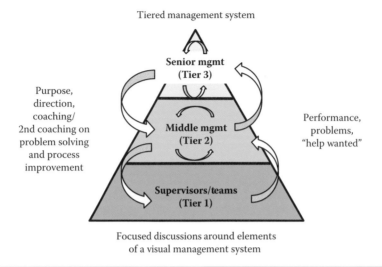

Figure 10.6   **Revised tiered visual management systems.**

development of leaders at all levels. However, we must provide a word of caution here. Leaders serving as second coaches must be careful *not* to usurp the responsibility of the one who is being coached to develop his or her own people. We've revised Figure 10.3 (see Figure 10.6) to show how this two-way dialogue should occur.

Examples of Tiered Metrics

We've just talked about the importance of including "tiered" process and outcome metrics as part of a visual management system and provided several examples. To recall, Tier 1 is typically the supervisor level; Tier 2 is middle management; and Tier 3 is senior management. It's very important to link the metrics between tiers and ultimately to a common goal or objective for the organization. Only then can everyone be assured that they are working together and moving in the same direction. We should also note that each tier of management has a different role to play in supporting the overall goal. For example, Tier 1 supervisors will focus on the process improvements that they can affect, such as reducing the time to process exceptions. They might do that by making exceptions more visible and making exception processing a priority within the department. Tier 2 managers will often focus on how to improve capacity and capability. They might do that by cross-training particular individuals between departments to process exceptions, or permanently reassigning or even hiring resources if such actions are deemed necessary. Tier 2 managers may identify policy changes to allow for exceptions to be processed in a timelier manner, or they might focus on the source of the exceptions if they originate in other departments. They would work to reduce the volume of exceptions rather than simply processing them faster. Tier 3 leaders are focused on the big picture, ideally on how to leverage the new performance capability to help the overall business, perhaps by growing that part of the business, or taking freed-up resources to offer new services.

Although it is impossible to provide examples for all processes within all industries and organizations, two additional examples are provided here for the reader's consideration. We hope that the examples spark ideas for specific metrics for your particular application. One example is for an accounting department, which most every organization has. The second one is for a hospital care unit.

Service Example: Accounting Department

Tier 1 Goal: Exceptions Resolved within the Week (Target or Service Level Is "by Friday of Each Week")

In-process metrics might include

- Volume of exceptions
- Progress against goal during the week (service levels met or missed)
- Reasons for exceptions (e.g., cause and source)
- Analysis of exceptions reasons, with suggested countermeasures
- Analysis of missed service levels with suggested countermeasures
- Progress on existing countermeasures against plans

Outcome/results metrics might include

- Percent of exceptions not resolved within the week

Tier 2 Goal: Reduced Exceptions, Improved Staff Capabilities, and Improved Efficiency in Processing Exceptions

In-process metrics might include

- Trends of missed service levels of front line performance
- Cross-training schedule showing performance against plan for improving skills
- Staff satisfaction scores
- Analysis of negative trends or unexpected outcomes (e.g., staff skills, more complex work, seasonal volume spikes)
- Suggested countermeasures to reverse the trends or improve against unexpected outcomes
- Progress on existing countermeasures against plan

Outcome or results metrics might include

- Productivity and overtime trends
- Freed-up capacity to do more work

Tier 3 Goal: Improved Productivity and Increased Service Offerings for Exceptions and Other Processing Functions

In-process metrics might include

- Productivity and overtime trends for all processing functions
- Capacity improvement trends and analysis for all processing functions
- Staff satisfaction trends and analysis for all processing functions
- Trends of service levels performance for all processing functions
- Customer satisfaction trends and analysis for all processing functions
- Trends of freed-up capacity improvements against anticipated capacity needed to offer new services
- Analysis of unexpected trends with suggested countermeasures
- Progress on existing countermeasures against plan

Outcome or results metrics might include

- Overall productivity for all processing functions
- Freed-up capacity
- New services planned or completed

Healthcare Example: Hospital Care Unit

Tier 1 Goal: Discharge Patients on Time with All Post-Discharge Instruction and Needs Met (e.g., Reconciled Medications, a Follow-Up Appointment Made with Next Caregiver, etc.)

In-process metrics might include (within each specific unit)

- Volume of patients
- Causes for missing expected discharge time
- Analysis and countermeasures for missing expected discharge time
- Missing instructions/needs on discharge
- Analysis and countermeasures for missing instructions/needs
- Progress on existing countermeasures against plan

Outcome metrics might include

- Percent of patients discharged within expected length of stay against goal
- Percent of patients discharged with all post-discharge instructions and needs met against goal

Tier 2 Goal: Discharge to the Appropriate Level of Post-Acute Care and Improve the Coordination of Care with Other Community Organizations

In-process metrics might include

- Trends in discharging patients on time with all post-discharge instructions and needs met
- Percent of follow-up appointments completed
- Percent of discharged patients following instructions
- Percent of post-acute caregivers following discharge orders
- Analysis and countermeasures for the aforementioned abnormalities
- Progress on existing countermeasures against plan
- Staff satisfaction scores

Outcome metrics might include

- Percent of coordinated handoffs by type (destination)
- Patient satisfaction
- Post-acute caregiver satisfaction

Tier 3 Goal: Improve Care Coordination Process and Reduce Avoidable Readmissions

In-process metrics might include

- Percent of coordinated handoffs for all care units and trends
- Patient satisfaction for all units and trends
- Post-acute caregiver satisfaction for all units and trends
- Analysis and countermeasures for negative trends on the aforementioned attributes
- Progress on existing countermeasures against plan
- Avoidable readmissions by source and diagnosis
- Analysis and countermeasures for avoidable readmissions
- Progress on existing countermeasures against plan

Outcome metrics might include

- Overall avoidable readmissions and trends
- Overall patient, staff, and caregiver scores for all care units

Summary

Leading an organization in a future state can be easier than leading it in the current state if

- Everyone knows what problem to solve (or not solve) at their particular organizational level
- What people focus on is clearly aligned to strategic needs
- People are allowed to be accountable for improving performance
- Reviewing performance is used as an opportunity to coach and develop the organization
- Visual techniques are used

The subtlety is that we can get there only by learning what works and doesn't work through trial and error, or experiments!

All that being said, every process, including the management process, benefits from continuous improvement. Approaching this improvement as a series of experiments designed to relieve an organization of the pressures of "getting it right the first time" and instead migrating to a great, adaptable system over time helps change the culture to one of deep understanding and commitment to performance improvement and staff satisfaction. This is a path with a deliberate design but adaptable execution, and we hope you are anxious to begin this critical dimension of your transformation. For more information on Lean management systems, readers can go to our websites and find newsletters, articles, and other materials on the subject. We wish you all the best on your journey.

Appendix I: Suggested Reading

Humble Inquiry: The Gentle Art of Asking Instead of Telling, Edgar Schein, 2013, Berrett-Koehler Publishers.

Note: A required read for anyone who wants to be an effective coach.

Lean Office and Service Simplified: The Definitive How-to Guide, Drew A. Locher, 2011, Productivity Press.

Note: Entire chapters on standard work, visual management, flow, pull, and leadership all in the context of office and services.

Lean Solutions: How Companies and Customers Can Create Value and Wealth Together, Daniel T. Jones and James P. Womack, 2009, Simon and Schuster.

Note: *Lean Solutions* provides more service-related case studies than its predecessor *Lean Thinking*.

Perfecting Patient Journeys, Beau Keyte et al., 2013, Lean Enterprise Institute.

Note: For those interested in the application of value stream mapping and management to healthcare.

Value Stream Mapping for Lean Development: A How-to Guide for Streamlining Time to Market, Drew A. Locher, 2008, Productivity Press.

Note: For those interested in the application of value stream mapping and management to development systems (e.g., product, software).

Websites

Beau Keyte, www.keytegroup.com.
Drew A. Locher, www.cma4results.com.

Note: Articles, newsletters, case studies and other materials can be found on the websites.

Appendix II: Demand Rate

For value streams that are transaction driven, additional analysis of demand may be needed during discussion of Future State Question 1. The team should ask

- What is the demand rate for the process? How much of the output is required over what period of time?
- How much does the demand vary over time?
- What resources will the organization require to meet the various demand rates?

In other words, the organization needs to know what the "takt time" is for transactional office processes. Takt time synchronizes the pace of processing to match the pace of customer need or demand. That is, takt time is the rate for completing work based on customer need. Takt time is defined as

$$\text{Takt time} = \frac{\text{Effective working time per time period}}{\text{Customer requirement during the time period}}$$

Let's say that in a single shift the organization can receive 46 orders. Order entry personnel work an 8½ hour shift with 30 minutes for lunch and two 10-minute breaks. Therefore, their effective working time per shift is 460 minutes. The takt time is

$$\text{Takt time} = \frac{460 \text{ minutes per shift}}{46 \text{ orders per shift}} = 10 \text{ minutes per order}$$

Ideally, order entry personnel should be entering one order every 10 minutes in a smooth and continual manner. Now let's say that the process time to enter an order is 20 minutes per order. The organization must provide two people to perform the order entry process to meet demand:

$$\begin{aligned}
\text{Number of people required} &= \frac{\text{Process time}}{\text{Takt time}} \\
&= \frac{20 \text{ minutes per order per person}}{10 \text{ minutes per order}} \\
&= 2 \text{ people}
\end{aligned}$$

This way, the organization can ensure that it is providing sufficient capacity to meet demand, and do so while fulfilling the defined service levels.

It is often necessary for the mapping team to define several takt times for office and service processes. Certainly, if demand varies, there will be multiple takt times. For example, an analysis of data at a call center revealed periods of high and low call volumes. Therefore, takt times were calculated for *each hour*. By comparing the takt time to the average process time for a call, the organization was able to determine the proper staffing throughout the day, hour by hour.

Remember also that we are designing a *future* state. Let's say that the demand on the value stream is expected to change in a substantial way in the future. The value stream mapping team must consider this as it goes about designing the future state. In other words, the expected future demand should be used for any takt time calculations that the team may make.

In addition, an organization can sometimes express demand in different work units. For example, let's say that the process time for an order entry process varies based on the number of line items on an order. Then line items should be used to express the demand on the order-entry process. The process time for order entry should be in terms of line items as well, so that an appropriate comparison with the takt time can be made.

Continuing with this example, let's say that the process time required to schedule an order is unrelated to the number of line items—an order is an order. In that case, the takt time for the scheduling process should be in terms of orders. However, later in the value stream, at the invoicing process, a team member points out that there can be several orders on an invoice. Here the demand should be stated in terms of invoices processed in a period of time, rather than orders. Then the demand rate can be directly compared to the invoice process time to determine the number of resources required.

What if there is no regular demand on a process? Can a takt time still be calculated? This situation arises for processes and value streams that are performed infrequently such as an annual budgeting process, or the month-end-close process that many organizations perform. Organizations can make use of the established service levels or goals for this purpose. For example, let's say that it is the goal to complete the month-end-close process within three days. And let's say that the total process time required to perform the various accounting activities that relate to the month-end-close process is 240 hours per close, per month. We will assume that the effective working time is eight hours per day, per person, and as mentioned the goal is to close in three days per month. Therefore, a total of 24 hours per month (8 times 3) is available. Using the equation below:

$$\text{Number of people required} = \frac{\text{Process time}}{\text{Available time}}$$
$$= \frac{240 \text{ hours per close per month}}{24 \text{ hours per month per person}}$$
$$= 10 \text{ people per close}$$

Therefore a total of 10 *full-time equivalent* people would be required to complete the month-end closing process by the three-day goal. A logical next question is "Who should do which steps?" A more detailed analysis could be performed by comparing the process time for each major step to the available time of the process (24 hours in this example) to determine the required resources to perform each. A graphical representation of this comparison is shown in Figure II.1. The comparison on the left side of the figure reveals that particular steps take longer than the available time (and service level) while others are well within.

With this information in hand, the value stream mapping team can reassign particular steps between resources to better balance the process and ensure that the goal can be met. This is depicted on the right-hand side of Figure II.1. Reconsidering current roles and responsibilities in the future state to improve flow and overall performance is common, and will be discussed in more depth when the value mapping team reviews Future State Question 3.

For purposes of Question 1, it is sufficient at this point to understand the overall resource needs and to identify possible "bottlenecks" or "constraints" that must be addressed in the future state. Consideration of demand versus capacity should be part of any application of Lean thinking. The team and the organization must be confident that the future state designed can meet expected demand and the goals defined.

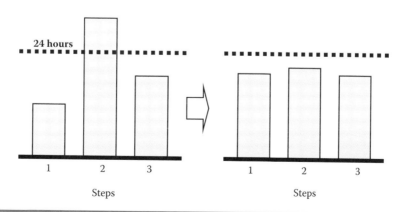

Figure II.1 Comparing process times to takt time.

One final note on takt time: the team will have been comparing the current state process times to the takt time, the available time, and/or the service level. What if there is substantial waste in particular steps in the current state? The team's focus will then move to addressing those wastes at the *key* steps in the process: the bottlenecks or constraints, or overall if a goal is to perform the value stream in the future with fewer people (which is not always the case). If the process times are expected to change (usually identified during discussion of Future State Questions 2 and 3), then the projected new times, *not* the current state process times, should be used in the analysis.

Index